Erasmus Wilson

The Eastern or Turkish Bath

Erasmus Wilson

The Eastern or Turkish Bath

ISBN/EAN: 9783337294458

Printed in Europe, USA, Canada, Australia, Japan

Cover: Foto ©Thomas Meinert / pixelio.de

More available books at **www.hansebooks.com**

THE

EASTERN,

OR

TURKISH BATH:

Its History, Revival in Britain,

AND

APPLICATION TO THE PURPOSES

OF

HEALTH.

BY

ERASMUS WILSON, F.R.S.

LONDON:

JOHN CHURCHILL, NEW BURLINGTON STREET.

MDCCCLXI.

PREFACE.

It is now about twelve months since, that my attention was first attracted to the EASTERN BATH. I thought I knew as much of baths as most men : I knew the hot, the warm, the tepid, and the cold ; the vapour, the air, the gaseous, the medicated, and the mud bath ; the natural and the artificial ; the shower, the firework, the needle, the douche, and the wave bath ; the fresh-river bath and the salt-sea bath, and many more beside : I knew their slender virtues, and their stout fallacies ; they had my regard, but not my confidence ; and I was not disposed to yield easily to any reputed advantages that might be represented to me in favour of baths. Mr. Urquhart talked to me, but without producing any other than a passing impression ; he had, many years before, illustrated, under my observation, the beneficial effects of heat and moisture on his own person ; but it bore no fruits in me ; for where could I find another man who would submit to a process of so much severity ? Without being prejudiced against the whole family of baths, I was not to be enticed into any belief or trust in them, without some posi-

tive and undoubted proof. Such was the state of
my opinion with regard to baths, when an earnest
man, with truth flashing from his eyes, one day
stood before me, and challenged me to the trial of
the Eastern Bath. I would, if no engagement
occurred to prevent me. " Let nothing stand in your
way, for there are few things of common life of more
importance !" was the appeal of my visitor. "On
Saturday, at four o'clock ?" " So be it." And on
Saturday, at four o'clock, with the punctuality of
Nelson, I stood in Mr. George Witt's Thermæ.

To George Witt, F.R.S., the metropolis is indebted for a knowledge of the Eastern Bath. Mr.
Urquhart struck the spark in " The Pillars of
Hercules ;" Dr. Barter caught it in Ireland, and
fanned it into a blaze ; another spark was attracted
by Mr. George Crawshay and Sir John Fife, and
burst into a flame in Newcastle-on-Tyne and the
North of England. Mr. Urquhart himself applied
the match in Lancashire ; but Mr. George Witt
introduced the Bath to London and its mighty ones.
Rank, intellect, learning, art, all met, as companions of the new " order of the Bath," in Prince's
Terrace, Hyde Park. And all will remember, with
kindness and affection, the generous disinterested-
ness and earnest truthfulness of their host.

When I stepped into the Calidarium for the first
time ; when I experienced the soothing warmth of
the atmosphere ; when, afterwards, I perceived the
gradual thaw of the rigid frame, the softeuing of

the flesh, the moistening of the skin, the rest of the stretched cords of the nervous system, the abatement of aches and pains, the removal of fatigue, and the calm flow of imagination and thought,—I understood the meaning of my friend's zeal, and I discovered that there was one Bath that deserved to be set apart from the rest—that deserved, indeed, a careful study and investigation.

The Bath that cleanses the inward as well as the outward man, that is applicable to every age, that is adapted to make health healthier, and alleviate disease whatever its stage or severity, deserves to be regarded as a national institution, and merits the advocacy of all men, and particularly of medical men; of those whose special duty it is to teach how health may be preserved, how disease may be averted. My own advocacy of the Bath is directed mainly to its adoption as a social custom, as a cleanly habit; and, on this ground, I would press it upon the attention of every thinking man. But, if, besides bestowing physical purity and enjoyment, it tend to preserve health, to prevent disease, and even to cure disease, the votary of the Bath will receive a double reward.

Having, in my own person, and in the experience afforded me by its regular use, become convinced of the power and importance of the Bath, I felt it to be a duty to make my impressions known to the Medical Profession. With this object I addressed an essay, entitled, " Thermo-therapeia, the Heat-cure,"

to the British Medical Association, at their meeting
at Torquay in August, 1860. In this paper, I
urged upon the members of the medical profession, particularly in the provinces and rural
districts, to erect a bath for themselves, as an
auxiliary armament against disease, as an addition
to their pharmacopœia ; and to give their support to
the establishment in every village and hamlet in
Britain of an Eastern Bath.

In September, 1860, I was invited to address a
paper on the " Revival of the Eastern Bath, and its
Application to the Purposes of Health," to the
National Association for the Promotion of Social
Science, at their meeting in Glasgow ; an abstract
of that paper will be found in the second chapter of
this treatise. And, having subsequently been called
upon to deliver a popular lecture at the Parochial
Institution of Richmond, I penned the historical
account of the Bath which is embodied in the first
chapter. This explanation I hope my readers will
accept as accounting for a certain degree of repetition which occurs in this volume ; and which,
without the devotion of more time to the labour
than I have at my disposal, could not be avoided.

It will be guessed, and with truth, that I am no
longer a sceptic of the value of the Bath, when the
Bath embraces the virtues which are possessed by
the Eastern Bath. That it is a source of much
enjoyment may be inferred from the suddenness with
which it has spread through the metropolis of

London. Turkish Baths meet our eye in almost
every quarter of the town, and three Companies
have been formed, or are in course of formation,
for the establishment of Eastern Baths on correct
principles. One of these Companies, under the pre-
sidency of Mr. Stewart Rolland, professes to draw its
inspiration directly from Constantinople, and will
take, as its especial model, the Turkish Bath.

When adopted as a social custom, the Turkish
model is clearly that which ought to be imitated,
on account of the moderate temperature which
belongs to it. The higher temperatures are upon
their trial; they are not a necessity of the process,
they may have their uses in disease; but it would
be best to treat them with caution, or, as a medicine,
leave them wholly in medical hands. The Bath for
the public should be one that they may adopt with
as much safety as the basin of water with which
they wash their hands.

The use of an elevated temperature is founded
on the well-known power of heat of destroying
organic impurity—such as odour, miasma, and animal
poison. But, in this acceptation, when applied to
the human body, it becomes a medicine of the most
potent kind; and should, therefore, be left to medical
management.

Henrietta Street, Cavendish Square,
March, 1861.

CONTENTS.

ILLUSTRATIONS.

CHAPTER I.

THE BATH, an animal instinct ; coeval with the earliest existence of man ; common to every rank ; a ceremony of his
birth, and a funereal rite ; discovery of thermal springs ;
the Scamander ; commemoration of the hot-bath by Homer ;
the hot-baths of Hercules ; estimation of hot-baths by the
Phœdrians ; frequency of thermal springs ; Hamâms of
the East, Hamâm Ali, near ancient Nineveh ; Hamâm
Meskhoutin in Algeria ; Baths of Nero in Italy ; German
thermal springs, Carlsbad, Wiesbaden, Ems, Aix-la-Chapelle ; the Geysers of Iceland ; thermal springs of Amsterdam Island ; of America ; of England, Bath, Bristol,
Buxton, Matlock . . . . pp. 1—5

xiv CONTENTS.

CHAPTER II.

REVIVAL AND SANITARY PURPOSES OF THE EASTERN BATH.

CHAPTER III.

RATIONAL USE OF THE BATH.

CHAPTER IV.

APPLICATION OF THE BATH TO HORSES AND CATTLE, FOR TRAINING AND THE CURE OF DISEASE.

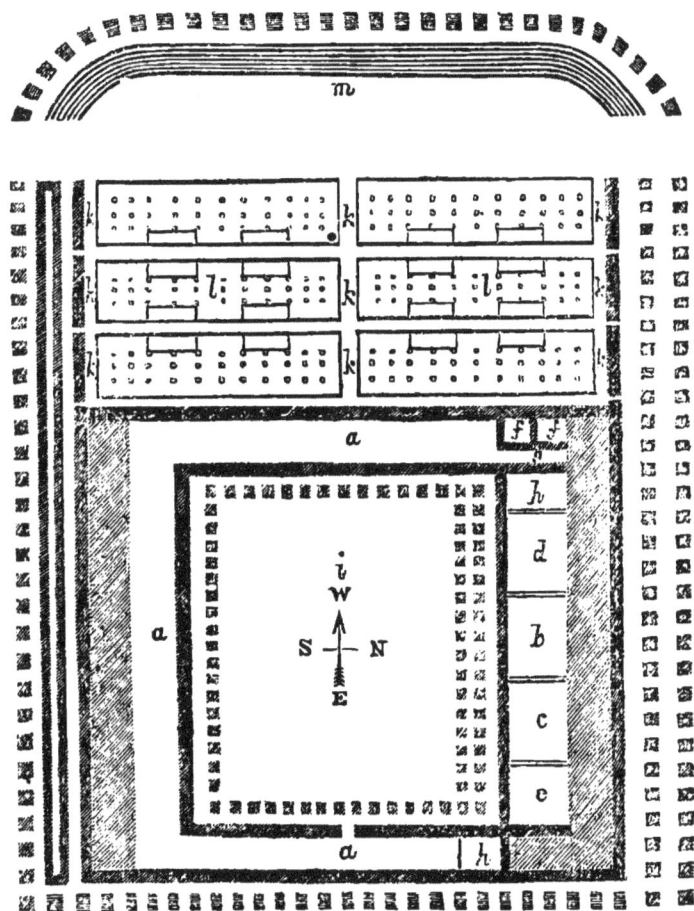

GROUND-PLAN OF THE PALÆSTRA OR GYMNASIUM, AFTER
VITRUVIUS. (Page 15.)

a a. The portico. *b*. The Ephebeum, the room of the Ephebi or
youths. *c*. The Apodyterium and Gymnasterium. *d*. The Elaiothesium,
or anointing room. *e*. The Konisterium, or dusting room. *ff*. The hot
baths. *g*. The stove or Laconicum. *h*. The cold bath. *i*. The Peri-
stylium or Piazza, which includes the Sphæristerium, and Palestra.
k k. Xysti. *l l*. Xysticus silvis. *m*. The Stadium.

PLAN OF THE ROMAN THERMÆ, FROM A DRAWING TAKEN FROM
THE WALLS OF THE BATHS OF TITUS. (Page 22.)

a. The Frigidarium, or cool room. *b.* The Tepidarium, or room of
middle temperature. *c.* The Calidarium, sudatorium, or concamerata
sudatio; around this apartment are seen several ranges of platforms of
marble. *d.* A vaulted stove, covered by an arched cover, *clipeus:* this
stove gave additional heat to the part of the room wherein it was situated,
and constituted the Laconicum. *e.* The Lavatorium or Balneum; there
are marble platforms in this apartment, and in its centre is an open bath,
called, from its large everted lip upon which the bather sat, *labrum.*
g g. The Hypocaustum. *h.* The room in which the water is stored and
heated. In the uppermost vase the water is cold, as is indicated by the
absence of fire beneath it. In the second vase the water is warm, being
placed at a considerable height above the fire. In the lowest vase the
water is hot. *i.* The Elaiothesium, or anointing room, from which the
bather passes to the Vestiarium or Spoliatorium.

THE HYPOCAUSTUM OF THE ROMAN BATH AT CHESTER. (Page 31.)

In the foreground are seen three of the short pillars or *pilæ*, with square shafts and expanded heads and bases. Between these more distant pilæ are visible, seemingly arranged in rows. The floor on which the burning embers lay is uneven; while the roof, which is the under part of the floor of the bath, exhibits evidences of the corroding action of the fire. The Hypocaustum, in the Roman Thermæ, occupied the whole of the under surface of the Calidarium, and the ruins bear evidence of the use of fires of prodigious extent.

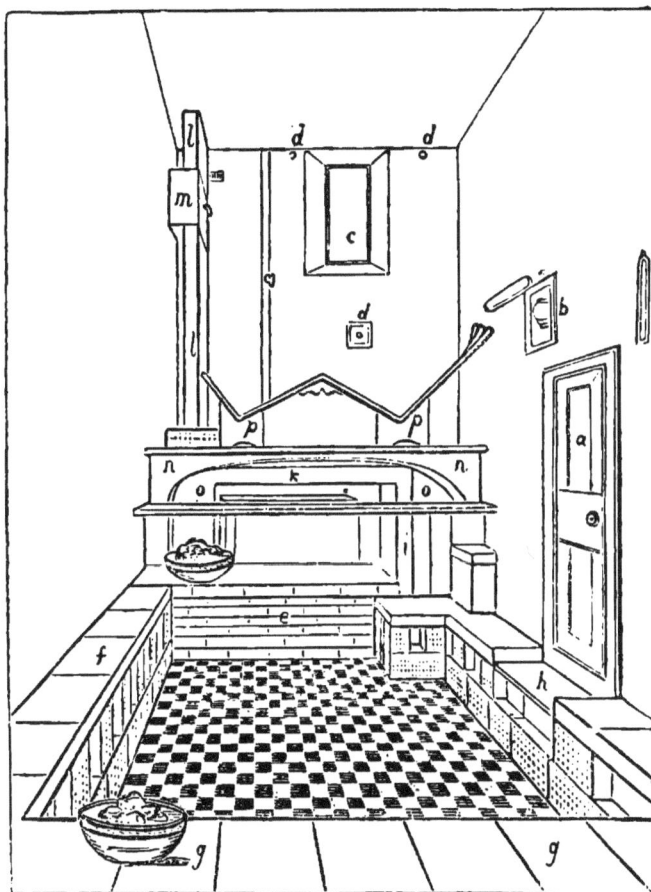

MR. GEORGE WITT'S BATH; THE CALIDARIUM. (Page 53.)

a. The entrance door. *b.* A small window looking into the Frigidarium; a gas lamp, for use at night, is seen through the pane. *c.* A thick plate of glass in the outer wall, for admitting light. *d d.* Ventilating holes; the lower one is furnished with a wooden plug. *e.* The masonry which encloses the furnace. *f.* The flue, proceeding from the furnace along the side of the room. *g g.* The flue crossing the end of the room. *h.* The flue returning along the opposite side of the room. *i.* The ascending flue. *k.* The flue crossing above the furnace, and then ascending, *l l,* the angle of the room, to terminate in the chimney. *f g g h,* support a wooden seat, on which the bathers sit; along the front of this seat, as at *f, h,* are perforated tiles and spaces, which give passage to the heated air. *m.* The warm water tank. *n n.* A platform, which also serves as a seat; the feet resting on the step *o o.* *p p.* The *dureta;* the letters are placed on the feet of the couch. The floor is tesselated; and on the seat are seen two wooden basins, containing soap and a bunch of *lyf.*

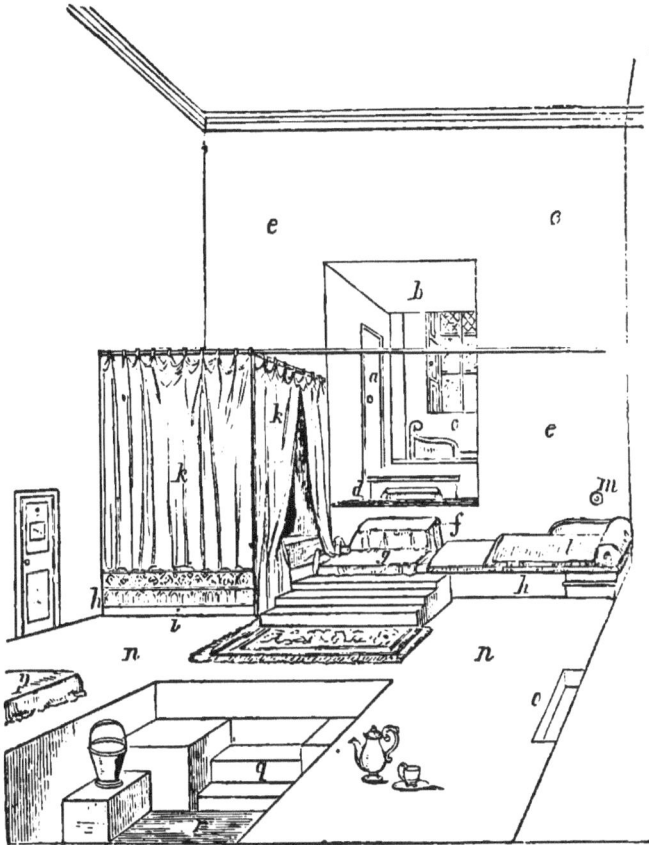

MR. URQUHART'S BATH; THE BATH AT RIVERSIDE. (Page 79.)

a. The door of entrance. *b.* The ceiling of the vestibule of the Bath. The side or rather the end of the vestibule *c* is occupied by an immense sheet of plate glass, through which are seen the Frigidarium, and the window of the Frigidarium, with a trellis of roses beyond. *d.* The floor of the vestibule. *e e.* One side of the great Hall of the Bath. *f.* A step covered with a Turkish towel. *g.* A platform, under which the hypocaust, *h h,* extends from one side to the other of the Hall. *i.* An ornamental grating, through which heated air enters the Hall directly from the furnace. *k k.* The tent, or enclosed chamber immediately over the furnace, where the highest degree of heat exists; the Laconicum. *l.* A couch, of lower temperature, but still hot, from being over the hypocaust. *m.* The spiracle of perfume from the mignionette bed. *n.* The floor of the Hall. *o.* The Lavatrina. *p.* A couch of less heat than *l. q.* Steps leading to the pool of cold water. *r.* The piscina or cold pool.

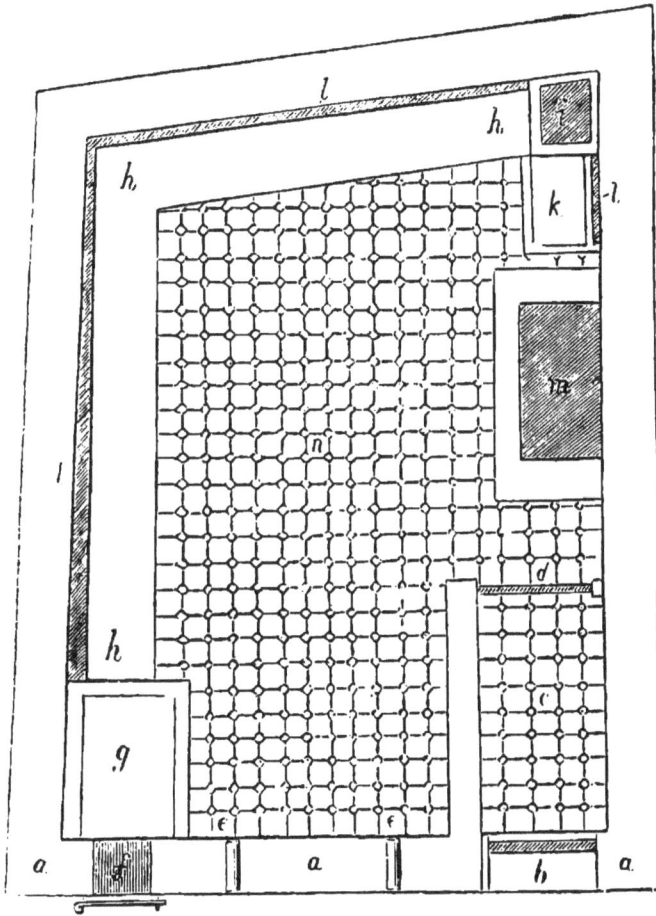

GROUND-PLAN OF MY OWN BATH AT RICHMOND-HILL. (Page 88.)

a a. Front wall. *b.* Door of entrance from a lobby, leading from the Frigidarium. *c.* Vestibule. *d.* Inner door. *e e.* Spiracles or ventilators. *f.* Mouth of the furnace. *g.* Furnace of fire-brick, enclosed in a jacket of hollow brick. *h h h.* Flue. *i.* Chimney. *k.* Returned flue, supporting a tank for warm water. *l l.* Outer wall; the dark shade between *l h,* and *l k,* indicates the interval between the flue and outer wall. *m.* The Lavatrina. *n.* Tesselated pavement.

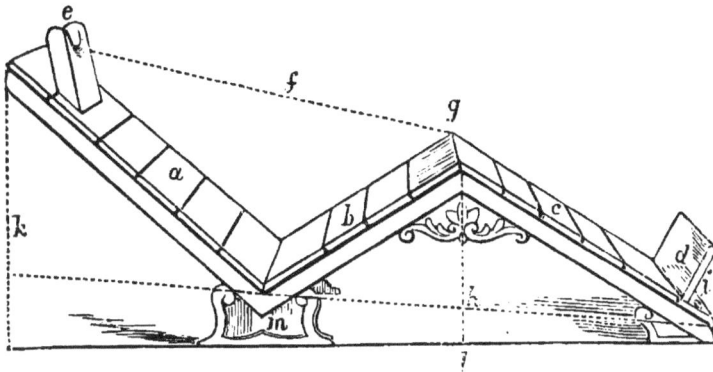

THE DURETA, OR RECLINING COUCH, USED IN THE BATH; BOTH IN THE CALIDARIUM AND FRIGIDARIUM. (Pages 53, 97.)

a. The plane for supporting the back. *b.* The thigh-plane. *c.* The leg-plane. *d.* The foot-piece, which is movable, and admits of adjustment, to suit the comfort of the bather. *e.* The head-piece, for supporting the head. *f.* Arc of the angle *a-b.* *g.* The angle corresponding with the bend of the knee. *h.* Arc of the angle *b-c.* *i.* Lower hole, for the foot-piece. *k.* Elevation of the trunk-plane from the ground-line, *l.* *m.* One of the feet of the couch.

This figure is intended to exhibit the construction of the *dureta*, the best lines of angle, and the size the most convenient for a person of medium stature—say five feet, eight inches. If the person be taller or shorter, a corresponding difference must be made in the length of the three principal pieces. The *dureta* is constructed of deal boards, 20 inches long, nailed on a pair of lateral rails; the rails being supported by a firm foot, *m*, and steadied by a bracket at the angle *g*. The measurements are as follow:—*a*, 28 inches; *b*, 18¼ inches; *c*, from *g* to the foot-piece, 19 inches; and from *g* to the extreme end, below the letter *i*, 23 inches. The holes for the foot-piece are two inches apart; and the head-piece may be made movable. The arc of the angle *a-b*, measured at *f*, from the upper angle of *a* to *g* is 38 inches; the arc of the angle *b-c*, measured at *h* from the angle *m* to the end of the plane *c*, is 37 inches; the height of the upper end at *k* is 24½ inches; the height of the angle *g* at *l* is 14½ inches; and the dotted line from the angle *m* to the perpendicular *k*, 21 inches; the height of the angle *m* from the point where the dotted line touches to the ground is 6¼ inches; and the height of the end at *i* is simply the depth of the rail—namely between two and three inches.

The *dureta* after the above model is manufactured by Mr. Allen, 7, Great Smith-street, Westminster.

THE

EASTERN, or TURKISH BATH.

CHAPTER I.

THE BATH is an animal instinct: and, *par excellence*, a human instinct; it is as much a necessity of our nature as drink. We drink because we thirst—an *interior sense*. We bathe because water, the material of drink, is a desire of the outward man— an *exterior sense*. An animal, whether beast or bird, pasturing or straying near a limpid stream, first satisfies the inward sense, and then delights the outward sense. A man, be he savage or civilized, can no more resist the gratification of bathing his wearied limbs in a warm transparent pool than he can resist the cup of water when athirst. Instinct bids him bathe and be clean. To inquire—Who invented the act of drinking? would be as reasonable as to ask—Who invented the bath?

The bath is coeval with the earliest existence of man. Can it be doubted that our first parents bathed their newly-created limbs in the river that

B

went out of Eden to water the garden"? History
teaches us, that the Phœnicians and ancient Greeks
of all ranks, from the daughters of their kings
down to the poorest citizens, were wont to bathe in
rivers and in the sea, for the purpose of cleansing
their bodies and refreshing and invigorating their
frames. They had recourse to the bath when they
ceased from sorrow and mourning, after great
fatigues of whatever kind, before and during their
meals, and at the conclusion of their battles.
Bathing was the first act of their lives, and it was
a part of their funereal rites. The birth of
Jupiter, the Thunderer, is celebrated by the poet
Callimachus in the following lines :—

> "As soon as you were born and saw the light,
> Your mother's grateful burden and delight,
> She sought for some *clear brook* to purify
> The body of so dear a progeny."

Again, of Alcestis, when about to lay down her
life for her husband Admetus, it is written:—

> "The pious dame, before the fatal day
> Of her own exit, bathed her beauteous limbs
> In *gentle rivulet.*"

Plato, also, records how the good old philosopher
Socrates, before he drank the fatal cup of hemlock
that was to consign him to Hades, *bathed* and *washed*
himself, that he might save the women, whose duty
it was, their troublesome office.*

* "Part of the funereal rites of the Moors was to convey the
corpse to the bath."—Urquhart, from "Mision Historial de
Marucccos."

A short stage in the history of the bath leads us to the discovery of springs of hot water, hot vapour, and hot air ; and these very possibly suggested to man's inventive mind the means of procuring so great a luxury by his own contrivance. Homer commends one of the sources of the Scamander for its warmth, and tells us how Andromache, with matronly care, prepared a hot bath for her husband Hector, against his return from battle :—

"Her fair-haired handmaids heat the brazen urn,
The BATH preparing for her lord's return."

We are taught also that Vulcan, or, as others say, Minerva, discovered certain *hot baths* ('Ηρακλεεα λουτρα) to Hercules, that he might replenish his strength after undergoing severe exertion and fatigue. And the Phœdrians, according to Homer, laid great stress upon the importance to the health and happiness of man of frequent changes of apparel, comfortable beds, and *hot baths*.

It is one of the marvels of the earth's history, that hot springs, or thermal springs, bubble upwards to the light, not only on Mount Ida, the source of the Scamander, but in countless other places and countries on the world's surface. These hot springs would appear to have invited man to their use by their pleasant aspect and by their warmth ; and their enjoyment to have suggested the possibility of contriving artificially a similar luxury nearer to his threshold.

The word Hamâm, which is equivalent to thermal springs, is not unfrequently met with in the East as the name of a town or village in or near to which hot springs are found. Hamâm Ali, in the neighbourhood of ancient Nineveh, is an example of this kind. "The thermal spring is covered by a building, only commodious for half-savage people, yet the place is much frequented by persons of the better classes both from Baghdad and Mósul."* Captain Kennedy, in his "Travels in Algeria and Tunis," tells us of the hot springs of Hamâm Meskhoutin, which rise to the surface at a temperature of 203° of Fahrenheit, only 9° short of boiling, and are so abundant as to burst forth through any opening made accidentally in the ground. "The thermal waters, in flowing over the bank of the rivulet, have formed a calcareous deposit of great beauty, resembling a cascade of the purest white marble, tinged here and there with various shades of green and orange."

In Italy, near the town of Pozzuoli, are some natural thermal springs—the ancient Posidianæ, now called the Baths of Nero, of which the temperature of the water is 185°, while that of the vapour which rises from it is 122°. The spring is situated in a rocky cavern at the end of a long passage formed by a fissure in the rock, and in this way constitutes a natural bathing house.

* F. W. Ainsworth: "Journey to Kalah Sherghat and Al Hadhr in 1840" (Transactions of the Geographical Society).

In Germany, among others, are the thermal springs of Borcette, with a temperature of 171°; Carlsbad, in Bohemia, 165°; Wiesbaden, Ems, and Schlangenbad, in Nassau; Baden-Baden; Aix-la-Chapelle; Wildbad; and Ischl.

In Iceland are the far-famed Geysers; in the Southern Ocean the hot springs of Amsterdam Island; and many more are dispersed over the Continent of America; while in England there are the thermal springs of Bath, Bristol, Buxton, and Matlock.

The *heated rock* and the *vaporization of water* would seem to have originated the primitive idea of a hot-air and hot-vapour bath; and this idea we find carried out simultaneously in various parts of the world and amongst the rudest nations. Mr. Gent, in his "History of Virginia," describes the hot-vapour bath as employed by the American Indians.

" The doctor," he says, " takes three or four large stones, which, after having heated red-hot, he places in the middle of the stove, laying on them some of the inner bark of oak, beaten in a mortar, to keep them from burning; this being done, they (the Indians) creep in, six or eight at a time, or as many as the place will hold, and then close up the mouth of the stove, which is usually made like an oven in some bank near the water-side; in the meanwhile, the doctor, to raise a steam, after they have been stewing a little time, pours cold water on the stones, and now and then sprinkles the men to keep them from fainting; after they have sweat as long as they can well endure it, they sally out, and (though it be in the depth of winter) forthwith plunge themselves over head and ears in cold water, which instantly closes up the pores and preserves them from taking cold." After the bath, they are anointed like the Romans, the pomatum of the Indians being for the most part bear's-grease, containing a powder obtained by grinding the root of the yellow alkanet.

But we find this primitive form of bath nearer home than the American Continent—namely, in Ireland, although both the American and the Irish bath may, Mr. Urquhart suggests, have been derived from the same ancestry—that of the Phœnicians. In a foot-note appended to a page on the universality of the bath, in his "Pillars of Hercules,"* Mr. Urquhart gives the following very curious and very interesting account of the practice of sweating employed in former times in Ireland, as reported to him by a lady as a recollection of her childhood :—

"With respect to the sweating-houses, as they are called, I remember about forty years ago seeing one in the island of Rathlin, and shall try to give you a description of it. It was built of basalt stones, very much in the shape of a bee-hive, with

* "The Pillars of Hercules; or, a Narrative of Travels in Spain and Morocco in 1848." By David Urquhart, M.P. 1850.

a row of stones inside, for the person to sit on when undergoing the operation. There was a hole at the top, and one near the ground, where the person crept in and seated him or herself, the stones having been heated in the same way as an oven for baking bread is, the hole on the top being covered with a sod while being heated, but I suppose removed to admit the person to breathe. Before entering, the patient was stripped quite naked, and on coming out, dressed again in the open air. The process was reckoned a sovereign cure for rheumatism and all sorts of pains and aches."

Dr. Haughton on the same subject remarks that : —"Two varieties of *Tig Allui*, or sweating-houses, exist in Ireland, one kind being capable of containing a good many persons, and the other only intended for a single occupant." The former is that just described : it is heated in the same way as an oven, by making a large fire of wood in the middle of the floor, and after the wood is burnt out, sweeping away the ashes. Besides the cure of rheumatism, the young girls who have tarnished their complexion in the process of burning kelp or sea-weed for the manufacture of soda, also resort to the Tig Allui for the purpose of clearing their skin. The usual time for remaining in the bath is under the half hour.

The second kind of Tig Allui—namely, that for the reception of a single person only—is described by Dr. Tucker, of Sligo, as follows :—

" It is built of stone and mortar, and brought to a round top. It is sufficiently large for one person to sit on a chair inside, the door being merely large enough to admit a person on his hands and knees. When any of the old people of the neighbourhood, men or women, are seized with pains, they at once have recourse to the sweat-house, which is brought to the proper temperature by placing therein a large turf fire, after the manner of an oven, which is left until it is burned quite down, the door being a flat stone and air-tight, and the roof, or outside of the house, being covered with clay, to the depth of about a foot, to prevent the least escape of heat. When the remains of the fire are taken out, the floor is strewn with green rushes, and the person to be cured is escorted to the bath by a second person carrying a pair of blankets. The invalid, having crept in, plants himself or herself in a chair, and there remains until the perspiration rolls off in large drops. When sufficiently operated on, he or she, as the case may be, is anxious to get out, and the person in waiting swaddles him up in the blankets, and off home, and then to bed. I have heard old people say that they would not have been alive, twenty years ago, only for the sweating-house. . . . . . Remains of the Tig Allui are also found in the county Tyrone, of the following dimensions :—five feet in height, nine in length, and four in width, being built of solid masonry, and shaped like a bee-hive at the top."

Another, and a very important step in the progress of the bath was the contrivance of a mode of
heating by means of which the temperature might
be made uniform, and might be regulated in any
manner that should be required. The hot stones
of the North American medicine-man were clearly a
very bungling and uncertain expedient; little better
than the warm skin of a newly-killed animal; and
the wood fire of the Irish sweating-houses was more
objectionable still, not only on account of the im-
possibility of regulating the heat, but also from the
resulting impurity of the atmosphere and the danger
of leaving fragments of the heated ashes on the
floor. The next contrivance, and that which has
continued to be the practice up to the present day,
was the construction of a furnace under the floor—
in other words, a *hypocaust.* Mr. Urquhart, speaking of the existence of baths among the Mexicans
and their probable introduction by the Phœnicians,
remarks:—" However magnificent their public
monuments," their baths were " such as are found in
almost every house in Morocco,—a small apartment
seven feet square, with a cupola roof five to six feet
high, and a slightly convex floor, under one side of
which there is a fire, and a small low door to creep
in by."

Reviewing the probable rise and progress of the
bath, there seems little doubt that the bath took
its origin in the East, the dwelling-place of our first
parents, the birth-place of civilization and know-

ledge. It was known at a very early period in
Phœnicia. Mr. Urquhart, in his recent work,
"The Lebanon,"* relates his discovery of a Phœnician temple, or crypt, among the ruins of Baalbeck,
or Baalbeth, *the House of Baal*—the Heliopolis, or
City of the Sun, of the Greeks; in which were traces
of the existence of the bath. "But the Phœnician
crypt was not my only discovery. In a gap opening a few feet into the masonry, I found mortar
hard as stone where exposed to the air, but soft
within. Yet it was unlike other mortar; it was dark
grey, with particles of charcoal; when I brought
out some, it was recognised at once, and called
kissermil, or ashes from the bath. Those ashes are
still used in this country for mortar, which with
this addition becomes as hard as stone. According to the old construction, the baths were heated
as an oven is, brushwood and dung being used as
well as wood. The combustion not being complete,
there remain various chemical compounds, alkali,
ammonia, sulphate and carbonate of lime, and carbon, which by entering into new combinations,
bind the mortar into a distinct substance."

"One thing is clear, there were baths at Baalbeck. In the elaborately finished bath of Emir
Beshir at Ibtedeen, one peculiarity struck me as
evidencing their high antiquity in this land. It
was the absence of cocks; instead of which simple

* "The Lebanon (Mount Souria): a History and a Diary."
By David Urquhart. 1860.

plugs or clots of cloth were used for the pipes which brought the water into the basins. As the Romans and Greeks used cocks, the art of the bath had not been derived from them, but traced beyond them. Still it was curious to observe these ashes in the midst of Cyclopic blocks. And yet why should not the bath have belonged to the very earliest period of human society ? It is sufficiently excellent to be from the beginning.''

" I remembered that in opening up the pavement of an ancient bath on the western coast of Africa, I had come upon a somewhat similar deposit, in large quantities, under the floor. This was *gazul*, the product of a certain mountain in Morocco, re- sembling soapstone, but composed of an admixture of silex, alumina, magnesia, and lime, and which has the peculiar property of polishing the skin when rubbed upon it, and so cleaning off the dead epidermis. Being used for this purpose largely in the baths, the grey deposit under the ruin in ques- tion is easily accounted for. Might not this same *gazul*, mixed with kissermil, have been the deposit which I took for mortar at Baalbeck ?"

For the purpose of removing the dead epidermis from the surface of the skin, " four processes have been adopted throughout the families of the human race, and in successive times. The simple, the natural, the first hit upon, was the rubbing down with the ball of the hand, which is still the process used in this country for currying horses of high breed. The three others, of a more refined and, I may say, historical character, are, scraping, rolling, and polishing. The scraping is with the *strigil,* which we know of from the Romans and Greeks, but which is figured on the tombs of Lycia, and the Roman name of which is derived from Mauritania. The rolling is that which we see to-day practised by the Turks. The polishing is with the *gazul,* and practised by the Moors, to whom it is confined, and who alone possess the admirable substance which is used for it. Now, if *gazul* was used by the early inhabitants of Baalbeck, their bathing process belonged to the last of these systems, and they carried on a traffic with Morocco."

From Phœnicia, from the coast of Tyre and Sidon, a knowledge of the bath may have spread along the southern coast of the Mediterranean, through Egypt, Tripoli, and Algiers, to Morocco and the Pillars of Hercules; or it may, as Mr. Urquhart suggests, have been earliest in use among the nations of Mauritania, and have been carried by the Moors into the countries of the East. From Phœnicia, the knowledge of the bath may have followed the line of caravan communication into Russia, Persia, China, and Hindostan; while the ships of the then greatest maritime country in the world would have carried it to Greece, to Ireland, and to America. The bath is a common practice in Russia; it is also well known in Persia, Hindostan, and China; and, as we have already seen, its

use in North America, in Mexico, and Ireland, probably dates back to a very early age. Its progress
in Europe we shall presently see.

Speaking of the mode of heating the bath in
Mexico and Morocco, I have used the word hypocaust; this word is of Greek origin, and signifies
under-fire—that is, the fire is placed under the thing
to be heated ; for example, under the foundation
of the bath or of the house. The Greeks and the
Romans had no other means of heating their houses
than this ; there was no open fire, but a fire under
the foundation, from which flues were carried upwards in the walls of the building. When a great
heat was required, as in the baths, the foundation
was supported on short columns (*pilæ*), and the entire space between the columns was occupied with
fire, while numerous ascending flues distributed the
heat around the rooms. Now it is curious to find
that at the present hour the Chinese continue the
same means of heating their houses.

That they also employ the sudatory process of
bathing, is shown by the following extract from Mr.
Henry Ellis's " Journal of an Embassy to China,"
published in 1817:—

" Near this temple (at Nankin) is a public
vapour bath, called, or rather miscalled, the Bath
of Fragrant Water, where dirty Chinese may be
stewed clean for ten chens, or three farthings ; the
bath is a small room of one hundred feet area,
divided into four compartments, and paved with

coarse marble ; the heat is considerable, and as the
number admitted into the bath has no limit but
the capacity of the area, the stench is excessive ;
altogether, I thought it the most disgusting cleansing
apparatus* I had ever seen, and worthy of this
nasty nation."

THE BATHS OF GREECE are celebrated for their
magnificence ; they formed parts of buildings of
vast extent and grandeur, termed Gymnasia. The
gymnasium was an institution of the Spartans of
Lacedæmonia or Laconia, and spread thence to other
parts of Greece, and notably to the metropolis of
Attica, the famed city, Athens. The gymnasium
was sufficiently large to accommodate several thousands of persons, and afforded space for the assembly
of philosophers, men of science, and poets, who delivered lectures to their scholars and recited their
verses ; and for the pursuit of the favourite games
and exercises of their youths and men—namely,
leaping, running, throwing the disc or quoit, and
wrestling ; the purpose of these exercises being to
give strength to the people and make them accomplished warriors.

The different parts of a gymnasium or palæstra,
were as follows :—

1. The PORTICOS, in which were numerous rooms

* What would Mr. Ellis say of a country in which there
existed no " cleansing apparatus" whatever?—for example, his
native country.

furnished with seats for the professors and their scholars.

2. The EPHEBEUM, a large space in which the ephebi or youths planned and practised their exercises.

3. The APODYTERIUM, or undressing room ; also called Gymnasterium, or the room for becoming nude.

4. The ELAIOTHESIUM, or anointing room, which was equally used by those who were preparing for exercise, and those who had completed their bath.

5. The KONISTERIUM, or dusting room, where the bodies of the wrestlers and other athletæ, after being anointed, were well dusted over ; probably as a defence to the skin against injury.

6. The PALÆSTRA, or wrestling courts, which were bedded with sand more or less deep, like the modern circus, in order to break the fall of the combatants when they were thrown to the ground.

7. The SPHÆRISTERIUM, or court for ball exercise and raquets.

8. The PERISTYLE, or PIAZZA, within which was the area of the Peristyle, for walking, and the exercises of leaping, quoits, ball, and wrestling.

9. Then there were XYSTI, or covered courts, for the use of the wrestlers in bad weather ; XYSTA, which were walks between walls open at the top and intended for hot weather ; and a XYSTIC SYLVIS, or forest ; the intervals of the numerous

ornamental columns of the building being so called, and being devoted to walking exercise.

10. Next came the BATHS, which were hot, cold, and tepid water baths; and a stove, or Laconicum, named after the city of Laconia and the Lacedæ-monians, from whom the Athenians derived their knowledge of the hot-air bath.

11. And lastly, there was the STADIUM, a segment of an ellipse, which received its name from being one hundred paces long, equal to six hundred feet, or something less than an eighth of a mile. The Stadium was furnished with rows of seats for spectators, and was intended for the exhibition of feats of running and exercises upon a large scale.

The most remarkable Stadium known was one erected by Lycurgus on the banks of the river Ilissus. It was built of Pentellick marble, and was so magnificent a structure, that Pausanias the historian, in describing it, informs his readers that they would not believe what he was about to tell them, "it being a wonder to all that beheld it, and of that stupendous bigness that one would judge it a mountain of white marble."

There were several gymnasia in Athens, the most noteworthy being, the Lyceum, the Academia, and the Cynosarges.

The LYCEUM, founded on the banks of the river Ilissus, was consecrated to Apollo; and not without reason, says Plutarch, but upon a good and rational account, since from the same deity that cures our diseases and restores our health, we may reasonably expect strength and ability to contend in our exercises. The Lyceum is also interesting to us as being the institution in which Aristotle taught philosophy. Aristotle was wont to lecture to his scholars while walking, and his disciples were therefore called Peripatetics ; he continued his teaching daily until the hour of anointing, which, with the Greeks, was a preparation for dinner.

The ACADEMIA was situated in the suburbs of the city, on a piece of ground that had been reclaimed from the marsh by draining and planting. It was called after an old hero named Academicus. Plutarch informs us that it was beset with shady woods and solitary walks fit for study and meditation ; in witness whereof another writer says :—

"In Academus' shady walks ;"

and Horace writes :—

"In Hecademus' groves to search the truth."

Plato taught philosophy in the Academia; but having in consequence of the unhealthy nature of the soil caught the ague, he was advised to relinquish it for the Lyceum. "No !" said the old man, " I prefer the Academy, for that it keeps the body under, lest by too much health it should become rebellious, and more difficult to be governed by the dictates of reason ; as men prune vines when they spread too far, and lop off the branches that grow too luxuriant."

C

The CYNOSARGES was also in the suburbs of Athens, not far distant from the Lyceum. It was dedicated to the god of strength, Hercules; and was interesting from its admission of strangers, and half-blood Athenians. Its name is derived rom the circumstance of a white dog seizing upon a part of the victim that was being sacrificed to Hercules by Diomus; and was the origin of the sect of philosophers known as the " Cynics."

BATHS OF ROME.—When Greece was subjugated by the Romans, the Romans carried back with them to Italy the taste for the bath. They erected thermæ of great magnificence, and in so great number, that at one period there were nearly nine hundred public baths in Rome. Agrippa alone is said to have built one hundred and sixty, while Mecænas has the credit of possessing the first private bath. The most famed of the public baths were those of Titus, Paulus Æmilius, Diocletian, Caracalla, and Agrippa. In these baths was centred all that was most perfect in material, elaborate in workmanship, elegant in design, and beautiful in art. Nothing was thought too grand or too magnificent for their decoration. Superb marbles brought from the most distant parts of the world; the choicest selections from the riches of their conquests, the curious and wonderful in nature and in art; precious gems and metals; and the finest works of the painter and the sculptor.

That beautiful production of the sculptor's art, the Laocoon, was discovered among the ruins of the Baths of Titus, and the celebrated Farnese Hercules in those of Caracalla.

The Baths of Agrippa were constructed of brick coated with enamel. Those of Nero were supplied with water from the sea, as well as fresh water. The Baths of Caracalla were a mile in circumference ; they possessed two hundred marble columns, sixteen hundred seats of marble, and were capable of accommodating nearly two thousand persons ; while those of Diocletian surpassed all others in grandeur, and occupied 140,000 men for many years in their construction.

Within the bath was collected all that contributed to the enjoyment, the luxury, and the gaiety of existence of the Romans. Here they practised their games, their athletic sports ; here they came to learn the news of the day, to listen to recitations of poetry and prose,* to hear the eloquent harangues of their orators, and to be entranced with the chords of melodious music. There were temples devoted to dancing, to refreshment, to the

---

* Pliny, in one of his letters, relates, in reference to the reading of poetical productions in the gymnasia :—"This year has proved extremely fertile in poetical productions: during the whole month of April, scarce a day has passed wherein we have not been entertained with the recital of some poem. It is a pleasure to me to find, notwithstanding there seems to be so little disposition in the public to attend assemblies of this kind, that the sciences still flourish, and men of genius are not discouraged from producing their performances."

bath; and in their abundant gratitude they raised
up appropriate statues to the gods who were sup-
posed to preside over their several enjoyments.
The great hall of their bath was ornamented with
the statues of Hercules, the god of strength;
Hygeia, the goddess of health; and Æsculapius,
the god of medicine.

It is not to be wondered at, that, reared in the
midst of the luxury, in the enjoyment of their
Balneæ or Thermæ, the Romans should have carried
with them their longing for the bath wheresoever
they went, wheresoever their victorious armies
forced themselves a way; and that, possessing a
mastery over England and Wales, which they
maintained for nearly four hundred years, they
should have founded baths in their chief settle-
ments in this country. Thus we have remains
of Roman baths in London, in Chester, in Bath, at
Wroxeter (Uriconium) in the neighbourhood of
Shrewsbury, at Cirencester (Corinium), at Caris-
brooke, in Colchester (Camulodunum), and in
several other places besides.

But here we are compelled to draw a line of
distinction between those grand institutions of their
own metropolis, which comprised, as I have just described, their places of recreation, of exercise, of
amusement, of diversion, as well as their temples
of health; which were, in fact, a centralization of
almost all the public institutions of their city into
one—and those particular parts of these insti-

tutions which were specially devoted to health.
Although the remains of the Roman thermæ in
England are large, although their construction
evinces a great perfection in many of the arts of
social life, particularly in the manufacture of bricks
and pottery, yet they scarcely bear* comparison
with the grander thermæ of ancient Rome, and
for this reason: that all that was simply ornamental—or, if I might be permitted to say so, that
was superfluous—has been omitted, and nothing
but the substantial and the wholesome allowed to
remain—that portion, in fact, which was purely
devoted to health and strength. We thus prune
the bath down to its simpler elements, and we
prepare the way for the consideration of the
bath as it has been revived amongst us at the
present day.

Without some explanation, it would be difficult
to understand how an institution which was regarded with so much veneration by ancient Rome,
should have totally fallen into decay in modern
Rome; and that the thermæ shall have ceased to
have an existence in Rome at the present day. It
is clear that the games which were once played, and
the exercises which were practised, within the narrow limits of the thermæ, grand though they were,
have now sought a wider sphere : the paintings of
their great artists have been gathered into the
ecclesiastical edifices and academies ; the statues
and sculpture have found their way into museums,

or have been applied to the decoration of modern palaces ; refreshment is more conveniently obtained in the cafés and restaurants ; music and singing have been transferred to the opera ; recitation to the theatre ; poetry and prose to the library ; and dancing to the assemblies ; nay, the great hall of the Bath of Agrippa is now, in all its integrity, a place of Christian worship.   In a word, the thermæ has become decentralized ; whether as the result of the adoption of foreign fashions, or as a matter of convenience, it may be difficult to say ; but so it is, and nothing of it now remains but the bath—that temple of the ancient thermæ over which Hercules, and Hygeia, and Æsculapius presided of old, and over which (in its humbler shape) they will continue to preside to the end of time.

The Baths of Titus have fortunately preserved to us a drawing, taken from its walls, which illustrates the construction and the mode of taking the bath among the Romans.

Beneath the bath is shown the furnace, or *hypocaustum*, for heating the rooms, as also the water used in the latter stages of the process.

Then follows a series of rooms, of which the principal are :—

1. The APODYTERIUM, GYMNASTERIUM, or VESTIARIUM : the undressing and dressing-room.

2. The TEPIDARIUM, which is warmed to a moderate temperature, and is intended to prepare and

season the body before entering the hotter apartment.

3. The CALDARIUM, or *Calidarium*, sometimes
called the SUDATORIUM, and in the figure (Fig. 2),
concamerata sudatio, was a room of higher temperature, in which the perspiratory process was accomplished. In this apartment there was commonly a
recess, of a higher temperature still, which was intended for special purposes, and was named LACO-
NICUM, in compliment to the Spartans of Laconia.

4. After the Calidarium followed a LAVATORIUM
(Lavatrina, Latrina), called in the figure Balneum,
in which the body was washed after the process of
perspiration was complete. The mode of washing
was to sit on the everted edge or lip of a large
marble trough—the *labrum*—and to be rinsed with
warm water poured over the body by means of a
cup or small basin (*pelvis*).

5. The bather then went into the FRIGIDARIUM,
where he received an affusion of cold water, and
where he reclined, or sat, or walked about, until he
was cool or dry.

6. From the Frigidarium the bather passed into
the ELAIOTHESIUM, or anointing room, where he was
smeared with fragrant oils previously to resuming
his dress in the VESTIARIUM.

Besides these, which were the principal rooms, there
were others devoted to additional processes, such as
shaving, hair-cutting, depilation, and hair-plucking.

The Romans carried the indulgence and decoration of their baths to so unreasonable a pitch of luxury and extravagance as to call forth State restrictions upon their use, and the reproof of their philosophers. Juvenal levels a shaft of satire against those who make the bath the instrument of gluttony; and Pliny scolds the doctors for declaring that the bath assists digestion, and for withholding their denunciations against its excessive abuse. Moreover, the Emperor Titus is said to have lost his life through excess of the bath, having spent in it many hours of the day. We cannot, therefore, be surprised that the time devoted to bathing should be limited by imperial edict, as happened in the reign of the Emperor Hadrian, the hours when the bath was open to the public being confined to two, —namely, from three until five.

PLINY the Consul, in his admirable letters, speaks in most affectionate language of the bath. " How stands Comum" (meaning Como, his birthplace), says he, " that favourite scene of yours and mine? What have you to tell me of the firm yet soft gestatio,* the sunny bath?" In another letter, addressed to a lady, he says:—" The elegant accommodations which are to be found at Narnia . . . . particularly the pretty bath."

Describing his winter villa, Laurentium, after painting a series of rooms, he continues :—

---

* A circus attached to Roman gardens, for riding or driving.

" From thence you enter into the grand and spacious *cooling-room* belonging to the baths, from the opposite walls of which two round basins project, large enough to swim in. Contiguous to this is the perfuming-room, then the sweating-room, and beyond that the furnace which conveys the heat to the baths. Adjoining are two other little bathing-rooms, which are fitted up in an elegant rather than costly manner : annexed to this is a warm bath of extraordinary workmanship, wherein one may swim, and have a prospect at the same time of the sea. Not far from hence stands the tennis-court, which lies open to the warmth of the afternoon sun."

" Between the garden and this gestatio runs a shady walk of vines, which is so soft that you may walk barefoot upon it without any injury."

Alluding to the mode of life of one of his friends, he observes :—

" When the baths are ready, which in winter is about three o'clock, and in summer about two, he undresses himself, and if there happens to be no wind, he walks for some time in the sun. After this he plays a considerable time at tennis, for by this sort of exercise, too, he combats the effects of old age. When he has bathed, he throws himself upon his couch till supper* time."

SENECA reproves the extravagance and self-indul-

---

* The state meal of the Romans, usually taken at the ninth hour—*i.e.*, three P.M.

gence of his countrymen in a memorable letter (his eighty-sixth), which is as follows :—

" I write from the very villa of Scipio Africanus, having first invoked his manes, and that altar which I take to be the sepulchre of so great a man.

" I behold a villa built of squared stone; the wall encloses a wood, and has towers after the style of a fortification ; the reservoir lies below the buildings and the walks, large enough for the use of an army ; the bath is close and confined, dark, after the old fashion, for our forefathers united heat with obscurity.

" I was struck with an inward pleasure when I compared these times of Scipio with our own. In this nook did that dread of Carthage—to whom our city owes her having been but once taken—wash his limbs, wearied with labour; for, according to the ancient custom, he tilled his fields himself. Under this mean roof did he live—him did this rude pavement sustain.

" But who at this time would submit to bathe thus ? A person is held to be poor and sordid, whose house does not shine with a profusion of the most precious materials, the marbles of Egypt being inlaid with those of Numidia ; unless the walls are ornamented with an elaborate and variegated stucco, after the fashion of painting ; unless the chambers are covered with glass ; unless the Thasian stone, formerly a curiosity worthy of being placed in our temples, surrounds the pools into which we cast our

bodies weakened with immoderate sweating; unless
the water is conveyed through silver pipes.

"As yet, I have confined my remarks to private
baths only. What shall I say when I come to our
public baths? What a profusion of statues. What
a number of columns do I see supporting nothing;
but placed as an ornament, merely on account of
their expense. What quantities of water murmur-
ing down steps. We are come to that pitch of luxury, that we disdain to tread upon anything but
precious stones.

"In this Bath of Scipio are small holes rather
than windows, cut through the wall, so as to admit
the light without interfering with its resemblance
to a fortification.

"But now we reckon a bath fit only for moths
and vermin, whose windows are not so disposed as
to receive the rays of the sun during his whole
career; unless we are washed and sunburnt at the
same time; unless from the bathing-vessel we have
a prospect of the sea and land. In fact, that which
excited the admiration of mankind, when first built,
is now rejected as old and useless. Thus it is that
luxury finds out something new in which to obli-
terate her own works.

"Formerly, baths were few in number, and not
much ornamented; for why should a thing of common life be ornamented, which was invented for use,
and not for the purposes of elegance? The water in
those days was not poured down in drops like a

shower, neither did it run always as if fresh from a
hot spring ; nor was its clearness considered a matter of consequence.   But, ye gods ! what pleasure
was there in entering those obscure and vulgar
baths when prepared under the direction of the
Cornelii, of Cato, or of Fabius Maximus?   For the
most renowned of the ædiles had, by virtue of their
office, the inspection of those places where the
people assembled, to see that they were kept clean
and of a proper and wholesome degree of temperature ; not of a heat like that of a furnace, such as
has been lately found out, proper only for the punishment of slaves convicted of the highest misde-
meanors.   We now seem to make no distinction
between being warm and burning.

"How many do I hear ridiculing the simplicity
of Scipio, who did not admit the day into his
sweating-places, or suffer himself to be baked in a
hot sunshine.   Unhappy man!   He knew not how
to enjoy life !

"The water he washed in was not clear and transparent, but, after rain, even thick and muddy.   This,
however, concerned him but little ; he came to the
bath to refresh himself after his labour, not to
wash away the perfumes of a pomatumed body.
What think you some will say of this?   I envy not
Scipio : he lived in exile indeed, who bathed in this
manner.

"Should you be told further, that he bathed not
every day—for those who relate to us the traditions

of early times, say that our forefathers bathed their whole bodies on market-days only—it will be answered, Then they were very uncleanly. How, think ye, they smelt? Like men of labour and fatigue.

"Since dainty baths have been invented, we are become more nasty. Horace, when describing a man infamous for his dissipation, what does he reproach him with? With smelling of perfumed balls! 'Pastillos Rufillus olet.'"

Of the ancient Roman bath in England, we have several examples, the most interesting being that which has been lately brought to light in the ancient Roman city, Uriconium, in the neighbourhood of Shrewsbury. Uriconium is close to the village of Uroxeter, commonly pronounced Wroxeter, five miles from Shrewsbury. It is situated on the property of the Duke of Cleveland, and is known to have existed at the beginning of the second century of the Christian era, when the Romans held dominion over England, and when England was a part, and a highly-treasured part, of the Roman Empire.

It was of considerable size, having a boundary wall three miles in circumference, and was, doubtless, a flourishing city; but fell a victim to the ravages of fire and the sword during the fifth century, and has since lain buried and unnoticed until the last few years, when a society was formed for the purpose of excavating it.

The walls of the houses are remarkable for their

thickness, namely, three feet; while that of the wall of the town is four feet. They are constructed upon a plan commonly adopted by the Romans—namely, a facing of stone on each side, and the space between filled in with rubble and that remarkable stone-like enduring mortar which has suggested the name of a better kind of cement of the present time, known as "Roman cement." The height of the houses was thirty feet; but they had no upper storey, and there is no trace of staircase.

Of the mode of warming the houses and, *par excellence*, the baths, the Rev. Thomas Wright* observes:—"The Romans did not warm their apartments by fires lighted in them. . . . The floor of the house, formed of a considerable thickness of cement, was laid upon a number of short pillars formed usually of square Roman tiles placed one upon another, and from two to three feet high. Those of the largest hypocausts yet found at Wroxeter were rather more than three feet high. Sometimes these supports were of stone, and in one or two cases in discoveries made in this country they were round. They were placed near to each other and in rows, and upon them were laid, first, larger tiles, and over these a thick mass of cement, which formed the floor, and upon which the tesselated pavements were set. Sometimes small parallel walls forming flues instead of rows of columns

* "Guide to the Ruins of the Roman City of Uriconium at Wroxeter, near Shrewsbury." 1859.

supported the floor. . . . . Flue tiles—that is, square tubes made of baked clay with a hole on one side or sometimes on two sides—were placed against the walls endways one upon another so as to run up the walls."

My friend Mr. George Witt, having recently visited the ruins of the ancient Roman bath still existing at No. 117, Bridge-street, Chester, describes it as follows :—

" The most interesting of all the Roman antiquities of this ancient city are the remains of a private Roman bath, showing the *Hypocaustum*, or heating place beneath, in a state of great preservation. The hypocaust is 18 feet long by 8 feet wide, and 3 feet high. The roof was supported on thirty-two stone pillars (of a single block), broader at the base and the top, and narrower in the middle; of these twenty-eight still remain. On the top of the columns are placed, by way of capitals, strong tiles from 17 to 23 inches square, and 3 inches thick, reaching from pillar to pillar, thus forming, at the same time, the roof of the hypocaust and the floor of the room above. Over all these is a bed of hard concrete, 9 or 10 inches thick, the whole suited to bear any amount of heat. The pillars are made of the red sandstone of the district, and are so far worthy of note, that they differ from the tile-columns of most of the Roman hypocausts found in other parts of England, which are chiefly formed of piles of 8-inch square tiles, 2 inches thick.

" The room above the hypocaust, which was the hot-chamber of the bath, called the *Caldarium*, has unfortunately been so dismantled, that little or nothing can now be learned of its character or proportions, two of the side walls only remain. The walls of these hot-chambers are generally lined on the inside by ranges of hollow flue-tiles, coming up from the hypocaust below, varying in number, according to the degree of heat required.

" There is nothing whatever here left of the *Frigidarium*, or cooling-room, nor any other of the apartments of the bath, nor of any of the contrivances used therein, except a sort of tank, 7 feet deep, 10 feet long, and 4 feet wide, situate near the mouth of the furnace, which may have served either as a receptacle for warm water, or as a place for a plunge in cold water, after the previous processes of the bath had been completed.

" Like modern Rome, the present city of Chester stands some feet above the level of the old Roman city; the visitors, therefore, must be prepared to descend into a dark cellar, to inspect the hypocaust and so-called bath ! and to emerge therefrom, with a bitter feeling of humiliation and regret, that our forefathers could have so ruthlessly destroyed these interesting evidences of the manners and customs of that wonderful people, who for upwards of four hundred years held dominion over this island—a people to whom we are indebted for the fundamental principles of our social civilization ; for the introduction of architecture, sculpture, coinage of money, construction of roads, and for innumerable other arts and adornments of life. There can be no more instructive proof of the mental darkness of those ages which followed the overthrow of the Roman Empire, than the wholesale destruction of the buildings of that great people, of which this is an example; and it is to be lamented that this barbarism, in regard to such monuments of antiquity, has not yet altogether disappeared."

And where, it may be asked, is the bath now; the conquering Romans have ceased to be other than a name, or a weary lesson for schoolboys; the Romans are gone, the Roman bath is lost. But here an eloquent modern author, Mr. Urquhart, helps us in our difficulty with a quotation:—"A people who know neither Latin nor Greek have preserved this great monument of antiquity on the soil of Europe, and present to us, who teach our children only Latin and Greek, this Institution in all its Roman grandeur and its Grecian taste. The bath, when first seen by the Turks, was a practice of their enemies, religious and political; they were themselves the filthiest of mortals; yet no sooner did they see the bath than they adopted it, made it a rule of their society, a necessary adjunct to every settlement, and Princes and Sultans endowed such institutions for the honour of their name." This, then, is the answer to the question—Where is the bath now? The ancient Roman bath lives in its modern offspring, the Turkish Bath—the Turkish Hamâm.

When, therefore, we see the words "Turkish Bath" in grand letters paraded through our metropolis ; when we see a human being performing the part of a sandwich, with a broadsheet of Turkish bath in front, and a similar sheet behind, himself representing a flattened anchovy between the two slices, we shall know that the ancient Roman bath, after being kept alive for many centuries by the fostering care of the Turks, has at last come back to revisit its ancient haunts, and to offer to modern Britons the enjoyments from which our forefathers turned away with contempt as a custom of their conquerors. And we are led to recognise the truth of my preliminary proposition—that the bath is an instinct, and that, being an instinct, its survival of a race is no longer a wonder, but is a law of nature —a law of the universe.

Let me now describe the Hamâm, or Turkish Bath as it exists at the present moment in Constantinople ; and in this description I shall take as my groundwork the account given of it by Mr. Urquhart. It is a large building, with a domed roof, a square massive body, from which minarets shoot up, and against which wings abut containing side apartments. The essential apartments of the hamâm are three in number—a great hall or *mustaby*, a *middle chamber*, and an *inner chamber*. We raise the curtain which covers the entrance to the street, and we find

ourselves in the *mustaby*, a circular or octagonal hall,
maybe a hundred feet high, with a domed roof, and
open in the centre to the vault of heaven. In the
middle of the floor is a basin of water four feet
high, with a fountain playing in the centre, and
around it are plants and trellises; and resting
against it, at some one point, the stall whence
comes the supply of coffee and pipes or chibouques.

Around the circumference of the hall is a low
platform, from four to twelve feet in breadth and
three feet high. This is divided by dwarf balustrades
into small compartments, each containing one or
more couches. These compartments are the
dressing-rooms, and the couches, shaped like a
straddling letter W, and adapted by their angles to
the bends of the body, are the *couches of repose*. It
is here that the bather disrobes; his clothes are
folded and placed in a napkin, and the napkin is
carefully tied up. He then assumes the bathing
garb; a long Turkish towel (*peshtimal* or *futa*) is
wound turban-wise around his head; a second
around his hips, descending to the middle of the
leg; and a third, disposed like a scarf over one or
both shoulders. Two attendants shield him from
view while changing his linen, by holding a napkin
before him; and when he is ready, the same attendants help him to descend from the platform;
they place wooden pattens (called *nalma* in Turkish,
and *cob cob* in Arabic) on his feet, and taking each
an arm, lead him to the middle apartment. The

wooden pattens are intended to protect the feet from the heat of the inner rooms, and from the dirty water and slop of the passages.

"The slamming doors are pushed open, and you enter the region of steam;" this is the *second chamber*, it is low, dark, and small; it feels warm without being hot or oppressive, and the air is moistened with a thin vapour. It is paved with white marble, and a marble platform eighteen inches high occupies its two sides, while the space between serves as the passage from the mustaby to the inner hall. A mattress and cushion are laid on the marble platform, and here the bather reclines; he smokes his chibouque, sips his coffee, and converses in subdued and measured tones with his neighbour. This is the *Tepidarium* of the Roman bath; here the bather courts a "natural and gentle flow of perspiration," and to this end are adapted the warm temperature, the bath coverings, the hot coffee, and the tranquil rest.

"The bath is essentially sociable, and this is the portion of it so appropriated; this is the time and place where a stranger makes acquaintance with a town or village. While so engaged, a boy kneels at your feet and chafes them, or behind your cushion, at times touching or tapping you on the neck, arm, or shoulder, in a manner that causes the perspiration to start."

After a while the bath attendant arrives; he passes his hand under the linen coverings of the bather ; if he find the skin sufficiently moist and softened, the bather is again taken by the arms, his feet are replaced in the wooden pattens, another slamming door is opened, and he is ushered into the *inner apartment,* " a space such as the centre dome of a cathedral," lighted by means of "stars of stained glass in the vault." The temperature of this apartment, the Calidarium or Sudatorium of the Romans, is considerably higher than that of the middle room; the atmosphere is filled with " curling mists of gauzy and mottled vapour," the steam being raised by throwing water on the floor. In the middle of the apartment is " an extensive platform of marble slabs," and on this the bather is laid on his back, his scarf being placed beneath him to protect his skin from the heated marble, and the napkin that served as his turban being rolled up as a pillow to his head.

The bather is now subjected to the process of shampooing—that is, his muscles are pressed and squeezed, his joints are stretched until they snap, and they are forcibly bent in various directions. In the hands of the professional shampooer the process is elevated to an art, and words fail to convey other than a very imperfect idea of its nature.

After the shampooing, the bather is brought to the side of the hall — around which are placed marble basins two feet in diameter, supplied by means of taps with hot and cold water—and made to sit on a board near to one of these basins. The

attendant draws on a camel's-hair glove. " He
stands over you; you bend down to him, and he
commences from the nape of the neck in long sweeps
down the back till he has started the skin; he
coaxes it into rolls, keeping them in and up till
within his hand they gather volume and length; he
then successively strikes and brushes them away,
and they fall right and left as if spilt from a dish
of macaroni. The dead matter which will accumu-
late in a week forms, when dry, a ball of the size of
the fist." In the course of his frictions he pours
water from the basin over the skin by means of a
copper cup, to rinse off the impurities.

In the next place, a large wooden bowl is placed
by the side of the bather; this bowl contains soap
and a wisp of *lyf,* the woody fibre of the Mecca
palm, and the body is thoroughly soaped and washed
twice over from the head to the feet, and, as a *coup
de grâce,* a bowl of warm water is dashed over the
entire body.

An attendant now approaches with warm napkins;
the hip-cloth, or cummerbund, is dropped, and a warm
dry napkin is selected to supply its place; another
is thrown over the shoulders, and the bather is placed
on a seat. The shoulder napkin is then raised, a
fresh dry one put in its place, and the first over it;
a fourth is wrapped around the head; "your feet
are already in the wooden pattens. You are wished
health ; you return the salute, rise, and are conducted by both arms to the outer hall."

In the outer hall, the bather is led to his box; he drops the pattens as he steps on a napkin spread on the matting of the platform; and he stretches his limbs on the couch of repose. "The attendants then reappear, and gliding like noiseless shadows, stand in a row before him. The coffee is poured out and presented; the pipe follows; or if so disposed he may have sherbet or fruit; the sweet or water-melons are preferred, and they come in piles of lumps large enough for a mouthful; and if inclined to make a positive meal at the bath, this is the time. The hall is open to the heavens, but nevertheless, a boy with a fan of feathers, or a napkin, drives the cool air upon him." The linen is twice changed; and when the cooling is complete, "the body has come forth shining like alabaster, fragrant as the cistus, sleek as satin, and soft as velvet. The touch of the skin is electric." "The time occupied is from two to four hours, and the operation is repeated once a week." At the conclusion of the process, "the crispness of the skin returns, the fountains of strength are opened : you seek again the world and its toils; and those who experience these effects and vicissitudes for the first time, exclaim—'I feel as if I could leap over the moon.'"

In reviewing the Turkish Bath and the process of bathing as pursued by the Turks, we are struck by several features which appertain especially to it : for example, its construction of three apart-

ments only, instead of the numerous apartments of
the Romans; the three apartments being, the grand
hall, corresponding with the Frigidarium of the
Romans, and being at the same time the Apodyterium and Vestiarium. Secondly, the presence of
vapour in the middle room, corresponding with the
Tepidarium of the Romans. Thirdly, the existence
of vapour in the third and inner room, the Calidarium and Sudatorium of the Romans. The presence of vapour betokens a low temperature, because watery vapour, as is well known, is scalding
at one hundred and twenty degrees of heat; and
we have fair grounds for concluding that there was
no vapour in the Tepidarium and Caldarium of the
Romans, and that the temperature of both was
considerably higher. For Seneca, in his celebrated
letter, speaks of the importance of maintaining the
baths at a "proper and wholesome degree of temperature; not of heat like that of a furnace, such as
has been lately found out, proper only for the punishment of slaves convicted of the highest misdemea-
nors. We now seem to make no distinction
between being warm and burning."—This criticism
would have been unnecessary had the bath con-
tained watery vapour, as the evil would then have
corrected itself, and the vapour, being scalding, could
not have been supported. Pliny also, speaks of the
"burning pavement of the floor" in his narrative
of an act of cruelty practised by the slaves of Lar-
gius Macedo on their master. After beating him

and trampling upon him, they threw him on the floor of the hot bath, and pretended that "he had fainted away by the heat of the bath."

Another peculiarity of the Turkish bath relates to one of its processes—namely, the absence of the cold douche with which the Romans concluded their bath. The Turks still dash cold water on the feet when the bath is at an end; but they allow the bather to enter the mustaby heated by the process and still perspiring—hence the necessity of a change of linen during the cooling, and the aid of an attendant with a fan to cool the body. Moreover, the process of cooling is in this way considerably lengthened, and we can comprehend how the bath may be prolonged to two, three, or four hours. In the Roman method—that is, concluding with a cold douche or a plunge in cold water—perspiration is immediately arrested by the closing of the pores, the body is cooled more quickly, no change of linen is needed, no fanning is required, and the cooling is accomplished equally well and in a shorter space of time.

The process of bathing, as pursued by the Turks, is also deserving of note. It is as follows :—Firstly, there is the *seasoning of the body,* in the accomplishment of which the skin becomes warm, soft, and moist. Then follows the shampooing or manipulation of the muscles, and stretching and playing the joints. Next comes the rubbing up and removal of the surface-layer of the scarf-skin. To this succeeds soaping and rinsing; and the process concludes with the cooling and drying of the skin.

"These are the five acts of the drama." The first scene is acted in the middle chamber, the next three in the inner chamber, and the last in the outer hall.

But that which most of all strikes us in the Turkish bath is the order, the decorum, the tranquillity, the dignity, the delicacy of the whole proceeding. A screen is held before the bather while he unrobes; his clothes are carefully folded and tied up; before he leaves the platform, he is clad in a becoming costume, which he retains till the end of the process, and he is guarded by similar decencies until he retires and quits the bath. This is the example which all true admirers of the bath hope to see followed in Britain : it is the Turkish bath which we seek to emulate, not merely in its construction, but also in its manners and management. There is one matter, however, in which we must fail—namely, in the multitude of attendants; but in this particular we must learn to do what we can, and not what we will.

Lady Mary Wortley Montagu has afforded us the rare opportunity of seeing the interior of a woman's bath in Turkey : her narrative, it is true, relates to the practice in 1717, nearly one hundred and fifty years back; but probably no great change has taken place since then. The bath she visited

was at St. Sophia, " famous for its hot baths, that
are resorted to for diversion and health." The
bath "is built of stone in the shape of a dome,
with no windows but in the roof, which gives light
enough. There were five of these domes joined
together, the outmost being less than the rest, and
serving only as a hall, where the portress stood at
the door. . . . The next room is a very large one,
paved with marble, and all round it are two raised
sofas (platforms) of marble, one above another.
There were four fountains of cold water in this
room, falling first into marble basins, and then
running on the floor in little channels made for
that purpose; . . . the next room, something less
than this, with the same sort of marble sofas, but
so hot with steam . . . proceeding from the baths
joining to it, it was impossible to stay there with
one's clothes on. The two other domes were the
hot baths."

The mustaby was already full of women, and
Lady Mary remarks on their good breeding. She
was dressed in a riding habit; "yet there was not
one of them that showed the least surprise or im-
pertinent curiosity, but received me with all the
obliging civility possible. I know no European
Court where the ladies would have behaved themselves in so polite a manner to such a stranger.
I believe, upon the whole, that there were two
hundred women, and yet none of those disdainful
smiles and satirical whispers that never fail in our

assemblies when anybody appears that is not dressed exactly in the fashion. They repeated over and over to me, *Guzél, péc guzél,* which is nothing but *Charming, very charming.*"

" The first sofas"—that is, the lower platform—
"were covered with cushions and rich carpets, on which sat the ladies; and on the second their slaves behind them, but without any distinction of. rank by their dress, all being in the state of nature, that is, in plain English, stark naked." There was as little to disturb them in that state as a group of naked children in the nursery; they had prac-tised the usage of the bath from their infancy, and the idea of indelicacy would no more have crossed their minds than it would that of Eve previously to her temptation. " They walked and moved with the same majestic grace which Milton describes our general mother with. There were many amongst them as exactly proportioned as ever any goddess was drawn by the pencil of a Guido or Titian— and most of their skins shiningly white, only adorned by their beautiful hair, divided into many tresses, hanging on their shoulders, braided either with pearl or ribbon, perfectly representing the figures of the Graces.

" I was here convinced of the truth of a reflec-tion I have often made, *that if it were the fashion to go naked, the face would be hardly observed.* I perceived that the ladies of the most delicate skins and finest shapes had the greatest share of my admiration, though their faces were sometimes less beautiful than those of their companions." The ladies were occupied " some in conversation, some working, others drinking coffee or sherbet, and many negligently lying on their cushions, while their slaves (generally pretty girls of seventeen or eighteen) were employed in braiding their hair in several pretty fancies. . . . They generally take this diversion once a week, and stay there at least four or five hours, without getting cold by immediately coming out of the hot bath into the cold room, which was very surprising to me."

This latter remark probably explains Lady Mary's refusal to take a bath with her companions. One of the ladies pressed her very hard, until she was at last forced to open her shirt and show them her stays, which, she says, "satisfied them very well; for, I saw, they believed I was locked up in that machine, and that it was not in my own power to open it, which contrivance they attributed to my husband."

Lady Mary Wortley Montagu also illustrates the extravagant decoration and expenditure that were bestowed upon some of the private baths even in Turkey, an extravagance that calls to mind the baths of Rome. Speaking of a bath she visited at Calcedonia, she observes :—" The baths, fountains, and pavements are all of white marble, the roofs gilt, and the walls covered with Japan china. Adjoining to them are two rooms, the uppermost of which is divided into a sofa, and in the four corners are falls of water from the very roof, from shell to shell, of white marble, to the lower end of the room, where it falls into a large basin surrounded with pipes that throw up the water as high as the roof. The walls are in the nature of lattices; and on the outside of them there are vines and woodbines planted that form a sort of green tapestry, and give an agreeable obscurity to those delightful chambers."

THE EGYPTIAN BATH is an offshoot of the Turkish bath; and the process, although somewhat different, preserves the general characteristics of its parent. Bayle St. John, in his "Village Life in Egypt,"* gives us the following sketch of the Egyptian Bath :—

"We went to the bath to be sweated and scraped, and rubbed and lathered and soused, in company with the respectabilities of Siout—brown-skinned, hairy, rotund gentlemen, who submitted to the operation with a gravity and sedateness at once admirable and ludicrous. Our presence, perhaps, put them upon stilts; but it was evident that, as they lay like porpoises about the slushed benches, enjoying a gentle titillation from the horny palm of the bath servant, or submitting head, back, and breast to the cunning razor, they felt what important people they were—citizens of a place which possessed a real bath, with *hararah*,

* 1852.

faskiyeh, and, above all, a scalding *makhtas*—the summum bonum of the Egyptian bather; for not all the race of Pharaoh bathe, as not all Frenchmen go to cafés, nor all Englishmen to clubs. From Cairo to Siout we had not found one of these luxurious establishments. In the antechamber, whilst we were being kneaded as if for dough by a coaxing lawingee, one old gentleman, who had doubtless been soaking for hours, came and sat down, wrapped in a sheet, opposite to us."

Mr. St. John fails to tell us to what extent he appreciated the bath; but Thackeray,* after a similar bath at Cairo, observes :—" The after-bath state is the most delightful condition of laziness I ever knew, and I tried it wherever we went afterwards on our little tour. At Smyrna the whole business was much inferior to the method employed in the capital. At Cairo, after the soap, you are plunged into a sort of stone coffin, full of water which is almost boiling.* This has its charms, but I could not relish the Egyptian shampooing. A hideous old blind man (but very dexterous in his art) tried to break my back and dislocate my shoulders, but I could not see the pleasure of the practice; and another fellow began tickling the soles of my feet."

M. Savary, in his " Letters on Egypt," published

* " Notes of a Journey from Cornhill to Grand Cairo." 1846.

† Probably the scalding makhtas of Bayle St. John.

nearly a century back, gives a description of the bath which is nearly identical with that of modern writers. The first apartment, he says, is "a great chamber in the form of a rotunda, with an open roof," and a fountain in the centre, which plays into a reservoir. "A spacious alcove, carpeted, is carried round, and divided into compartments, in which the bathers leave their clothes," and to which they return when the bath is over. When undressed, "sandals are put on, and a narrow passage is entered, where the heat first begins to be felt; the door shuts, and twenty paces further a second opens, which is the entrance to a passage at right angles with the first. Here the heat augments, and those who fear to expose themselves too suddenly to its effects, stop some time in a marble hall (middle chamber) before they enter. The bath itself (inner chamber) is a spacious vaulted chamber, paved and lined with marble; beside it are four small rooms: a vapour continually rises from a fountain and cistern of hot water, with which the burnt perfumes mingle."

His notice of the process of shampooing differs somewhat from that of others:—"A gentle moisture diffuses itself over the body; a servant comes, gently presses and turns the bather, and when the limbs are flexible, makes the joints crack without trouble, then *masses* (touches lightly), and seems to knead the body without giving the slightest sensation of pain.

"This done, he puts on a stuff glove, and continues rubbing long," until the skin "becomes as smooth as satin; he then conducts the bather into a cabinet, pours a lather of perfumed soap on the head, and retires." "The room into which the bather retires has two water-cocks—one for cold, the other for hot water; and he washes himself."

"Being well washed and purified, the bather is wrapped up in hot linen. Being come to the alcove, a bed is ready prepared, on which the person no sooner lies down, than a boy comes, and begins to press with his delicate hands all parts of the body, in order to dry them perfectly; the linen is once more changed, and the boy gently rubs the callous skin of the feet with pumice stone, then brings a pipe and Mocha coffee."

M. Savary then draws the following picture of the sensations of the bath:—"Coming from a bath filled with hot vapour, in which excessive perspiration bedewed every limb, into a spacious apartment and the open air, the lungs expand and respire at pleasure: well kneaded, and, as it were, regenerated, the blood circulates freely, the body feels a voluptuous ease, a flexibility till then unknown, a lightness as if relieved from some enormous weight, and the man almost fancies himself newly-born and beginning first to live. A glowing consciousness of existence diffuses itself to the very extremities; and, while thus yielding to the most delightful sensations, ideas of the most pleasing kind pervade and fill the soul; the imagination wanders through worlds which itself embellishes, everywhere drawing pictures of happiness and delight. If life be only a succession of ideas, the vigour, the rapidity with which the memory then retraces all the knowledge of the man would lead us to believe that the two hours of delicious calm which succeed bathing are an age.

"Such, sir, are these baths, the use of which was so strongly recommended by the ancients, and the pleasures of which the Egyptians still enjoy. Here they prevent or exterminate rheumatisms, catarrhs, and those diseases of the skin which the want of perspiration occasions. Here they rid themselves of those uncomfortable sensations so common among other nations, who have not the same regard to cleanliness."*

With the Turkish bath for our model, let us now inquire—What the bath has been doing in Britain? and, How a desire to restore it first came among us? That it is among us is a fact beyond question, and that it has spread through society with marvellous rapidity no longer admits of doubt. In the year 1850, Mr. Urquhart pub-

---

* "Tournefort, who had taken the vapour baths at Constantinople, where they are much less careful than at Grand Cairo, thinks they injure the lungs; but longer experience would have convinced him of his error. There are no people who practise this bathing more than the Egyptians, nor any to whom such diseases are less known. They are almost wholly unacquainted with pulmonic complaints."

lished an interesting work in two volumes, entitled "The Pillars of Hercules; or, a Narrative
of Travels in Spain and Morocco in 1848." In
the preface to this work occurs the following passage :—" I have no expectation that my suggestions
will modify the lappet of a coat, or the leavening
of a loaf; but there is one subject in which I am
not without hope of having placed a profitable
habit more within the chance of adoption than it
has hitherto been—I mean the bath." In the
second volume of this work there is a chapter
(Chapter VIII.) devoted to the bath, and especially to a description of the Turkish and Moorish
bath. It is from this source that I have drawn
the description which I have just given ; and the
author refers to it in the conclusion of his seventh
chapter in these words:—" A chapter," says he,
" which, if the reader will peruse it with diligence
and apply with care, may prolong his life, fortify
his body, diminish his ailments, augment his enjoyments, and improve his temper ; then, having found
something beneficial to himself, he may be prompted
to do something to secure the like for his fellow-
creatures."

Six years after the publication of this work—
namely, in 1856—Mr. Urquhart visited Ireland,
and made the acquaintance of Dr. Richard Barter,
the proprietor of a water-cure establishment at
Blarney. Dr. Barter, struck with the conversation of Mr. Urquhart, and delighted with his de-

scription of the Turkish bath, which he subsequently read in the "Pillars of Hercules," wrote to him as follows:—" Your description of the Turkish bath has electrified me. If you will come down here and superintend the erection of one, men, money, and materials shall be at your disposal."

Mr. Urquhart, in his zeal for the cause, on which he has so ably and so eloquently written, accepted the invitation, and a month later, the foundation-stone of the Turkish Bath of St. Anne's Hill, Blarney—the parent of numerous baths which have since sprung into existence in Ireland—was laid.

The chiefs of the pioneers of the Bath in England, following the teachings of Mr. Urquhart, are, Mr. George Crawshay, Sir John Fife, Mr. George Witt, and Mr. Stewart Rolland. The first private bath erected in England was that of Mr. Crawshay, in 1857. In the same year, Mr. Urquhart constructed a small bath at his residence at Lytham, and the year following commenced his elegant bath at Riverside. Mr. Witt followed in 1858, and Mr. Rolland in 1859. It was in Mr. Witt's bath that I first took rank as a bather, and on that account, as well as for its comfort and simplicity, and the philanthropic character of its owner, Mr. Witt's bath will always occupy a first place both in my memory and in my heart. Let me describe it.

On the ground-floor of his house in Prince's Terrace, Hyde Park, is a room twenty feet long by ten feet in breadth, and twelve feet high, with a window looking out upon a lead-flat. This room he divided by a partition into two' compartments, two-thirds of the room being devoted to the purposes of a cool-room, and the remaining third to a hot-room. The outer room being the Mustaby or Frigidarium; the inner room being the hot-room of the. Turkish Hamâm, the Calidarium and Sudatorium of the Romans; there was no space for a middle room, or Tepidarium.

Piercing the wall of the Calidarium near its floor is a furnace of simple construction, opening on the lead-flat outside, and projecting for some distance inside into the room, where it is covered with a casing of fire-brick; the furnace ends in a flue, and the flue, which is one foot square, runs around the room, close to the floor, and close also to the wall, being separated from both the one and the other by a space of a few inches. Having completed the circuit of the room, the flue ascends the angle of the apartment to the ceiling, and terminates by opening into a chimney-shaft. The room is heated by the radiation of caloric from the casing of the furnace, and from the flue; and the flue being thirty-five feet in length, presents a radiating surface of nearly fifty yards.

The other features in the construction of the Calidarium are, a wooden seat, which runs round the room, immediately over the flue; a platform which supports a *dureta*, or couch of repose; a

small tank holding ten gallons of water, kept warm
by its position against the chimney-shaft, and two
pipes which project into the room, at an elevation
of six feet and a half, for supplying warm water
from the tank, and cold water from the ordinary
house-service; add to this a double door of entrance,
a small window, and five circular holes in the wall
for ventilation, and the Calidarium is complete.

Let me now conduct the reader through the process of taking a bath.

We enter the Frigidarium ; we divest ourselves
of our clothing, which we hang on pegs fixed along
the end of the room ; this is the Vestiarium, or
Apodyterium ; and here we put off our shoes. We
then dress ourselves for the bath : we wind a long
strip of Turkish red twilled cotton around our hips,
in the fashion of a cummerbund or kilt ; it descends
nearly to our knees ; we fold another strip turban-
wise around our head; and behold! we are ready
to enter the region of heat. We need no wooden
pattens, no *cob cob ;* on the clean India matting of
the Frigidarium, where shoe-leather never treads,
there is no dust; on the floor of the Calidarium
we shall find neither slop nor excessive heat; we
may press our naked sole against Mother Earth as
we would press palm to palm with our dearest
friend.

The question of precedence being settled, the
double door is opened, and we enter the Calidarium.
How deliciously the warm air seems to fold us in

its soft embrace; we look at the thermometer:
it is 135°. How very nice! How very agreeable!
are the expressions which we hear softly breathed
around us, for we are not alone : we are one of five
or six " Companions of the Bath." The air is clear
—no vapoury mists; it is fresh, for there is a free
circulation of air through the room; but how mar-
vellously soothing! All care, all anxiety, all
trouble, all memory of the external world and its
miserable littleness, is chased from the mind; our
thoughts are absorbed in rapturous contemplation
of the delights of the New World—the Paradise
into which we have just been admitted. The
tyrant PAIN, even, loses his miscreant power here;
the toothache, where is it gone? the headache, gone
too; the spasm no longer bides; the grinding aches
of craving appetite, the pang of neuralgia, of
rheumatism, of gout—all are fled; for this is the
region where the suffering find a soothing relief
from all their torments; and over the door is it
not written:—THIS IS THE CALIDARIUM; PAIN
ENTERS NOT HERE.

Ten minutes slip away in an enjoyment that
seems to last for a lifetime; and what is our condition now? The skin is warm, it is soft, it is
moist, for sensible perspiration has commenced.
Those parts perspire first which have been most
exposed to the air—namely, the forehead, the head,
the neck, the chest and shoulders, because these
parts, from that very exposure, are in the most

normal state. We are shortly, "like Niobe, all tears;" but our tears are tears of bliss. Tears of perspiration collect in beads at the apertures of the pores; tears glide down the surface, and fall from all the salient points of our frame, from our elbows, from our finger-ends; a sweet languor creeps over us, and we feel as though, like a heathen god of old, we were dissolving into a liquid stream.

"Here Fluvius wept; as now a stream declares."

We experience the truth of the saying of Sanctorius, "that melancholy is overcome by a free perspiration, and that cheerfulness, without any evident cause, proceeds from perspiration succeeding well."

It is a curious, but at the same time an obvious fact, with regard to perspiration, that it depends very materially on the habit and training of the skin. The beginner in the use of the bath perspires slowly, languidly, partially, incompletely, while the accustomed bather is known by the freedom of his perspiration. The apprentice-hand has no thirst in the bath, for a small portion only of the excess of watery fluid is abstracted from his tissues and from his blood. But the practised bather has no such excess, his blood yields its diluting water with great freedom, he thirsts in the bath, and he drinks freely. I know a gentleman who sometimes consumes a gallon of water in the bath, but none remains when he comes out: all has been dissipated by perspiration. In a chemical analysis of the perspiration of a group of bathers, recently made, that fluid was found loaded with saline and organic matter in the recruits, but was almost pure in the veteran bather : his blood was washed as clean as that of the working man who eats the bread of labour—that sweetest of all bread, the bread that has been earned with the sweat of his brow.

I hardly know a more curious or more beautiful sight than that of the healthy skin of a practised bather, spangled over with limpid drops of perspiration like dew-drops on the petals of a rose, or like beads of crystal, as I heard a Doctor of Divinity once call them, in the bath. The Reverend Doctor, although a distinguished member of the Protestant Church, was, as a witty friend remarked, " devoutly counting his beads."

Among the labourers in hot rooms, or in proximity with hot furnaces, as in the manufacture of glass, enamel, porcelain, and gas, the working of engines, and the smelting of metals, perspiration is very profuse, and the lost fluid is replaced by the drinking of water, or more commonly of thin gruel; restoring the balance of fluids not by mere water, but actually by a nutritive drink. Look at these men, working in the open air, or in the midst of thorough draughts, with rivers of perspiration streaming down their athletic frames, and ask their history ; they are healthy, long-lived, and happy.

In the copper-smelting works at Swansea, the heat between the furnaces at which the men work is 200° of Fahrenheit; they drink a gallon of thin gruel every hour, working four hours at a stretch, and the ground on which they stand is a pool of perspiration.

I have said that the temperature of Mr. Witt's bath is 135°, and a very agreeable temperature it is ; but the temperature of the bath is a point upon which a few observations must be made. The temperature of the Calidarium in Mr. Urquhart's and Mr. Rolland's bath is 170°, and is equally agreeable, equally fresh, equally enjoyable. What then, it may be asked, is the difference between these baths, that renders such a wide range of temperature equally pleasant ? It is one of construction. Mr. Witt's Calidarium is small, well ventilated for its size, but a higher temperature than 135° or 140° would be oppressive if more than two or three bathers were present. Moreover, in Mr. Witt's bath, there is an invisible vapour of water in suspension in the atmosphere. Mr. Rolland's bath is larger than Mr. Witt's, and the atmosphere perfectly dry. Size of apartment and dryness of atmosphere are therefore the opposites of restricted space and moist atmosphere. Mr. Urquhart's bath, with a higher temperature than Mr. Rolland's, is fresher than either, because he has been enabled to combine greater size, greater altitude, a fresher material, namely, marble, moisture, and partial heating by means of the hypocaust. So the question of temperature must be regarded as relative, and not positive ; a higher temperature will be fresher in a large and well-ventilated bath with few inmates, than a lower temperature in a small and less perfectly ventilated apartment. Whereas, the bath that may be fresh and agreeable in the morning when few bathers are present, may be insufferable in the after part of the day when a succession of bathers has rendered the atmosphere moist, or when many bathers are therein. The effect of many bathers being necessarily to curtail space, infuse moisture into the atmosphere, and deteriorate the ventilating medium. The temperature of a bath must therefore be specially adapted to the particular bath ; it must rise or fall with its proportions or with its means of ventilation ; it must rise or fall with its number of bathers ; it must rise in the morning and fall in the evening. We may fix the temperature of a hot bath, but we cannot determine that of a Turkish bath.

One of the things which strikes the popular mind the most vividly in the British Turkish bath is the *high temperature.* When we call to mind that a hot bath is scalding at 110°, and a vapour bath at 120°, we are astonished to hear of a bath that is enjoyable at 20°, 30°, and even 50° above the temperature of scalding water. Nay, more, that can be borne without inconvenience at *double* the temperature of scalding water. Mr. Witt, one evening at a dinner-party, explained the curious difference of action of heat on living and dead organic matter. A few days after, a baronet, who was one of the party, visited Mr. Witt in his bath, and wrote to an incredulous friend as follows :— "I have been at Mr. Witt's bath ; all that he told us is true. I cooked a mutton-chop on my knee ! and in eating it afterwards the only inconvenience that I experienced was in the matter of the bread— it became toast before I could get it to my mouth." Since I first published this anecdote, a very matter-of-fact gentleman has written to me to say : "Well! I can believe the mutton-chop, but is not the bread changing to toast in its way to the mouth a little too much for credit ?" I can best answer my matter-of-fact friend by saying, that in Mr. Urquhart's bath at Riverside, I sat for at least ten minutes, and without the slightest inconvenience, in his Laconicum, at a temperature of 240°—namely, 28° degrees above the boiling-point of water. If I had had bread, or meat, or eggs with me, they must necessarily have been cooked at that heat. But in reality there is nothing wonderful in all this. I am informed that during the Indian mutiny, the heat in the tents was sometimes as high as 140°. Sir Charles Blagden remained for ten minutes in a room heated to 260°. Sir Francis Chantrey's oven, in which his moulds were dried, and which was con-stantly entered by his men, was heated to 350°. The ovens in the slate-enamelling works of Mr.

Magnus, at Pimlico, also habitually entered by the workmen, have a temperature of 350°. And the oven in which Chabert, the so-called Fire King, exhibited in London some years back, was heated to 400° and 500°.

We may therefore pass over the bravery of the exceeding high temperatures as an established fact, and not worthy of a single further remark. Man, who would be scalded by water at a temperature of 110°, and vapour or steam at 120°, can bear for a short time dry air at a temperature of 500° of Fahrenheit, and upwards. But this does not so much concern us as the question—WHAT IS THE BEST TEMPERATURE OF BATH, FOR THE PURPOSES OF HEALTH? My answer must be, a moderate temperature—a temperature ranging in medium limits between 120° and 140°. The Romans, who lost the bath, used very high temperatures; the Turks, who have preserved it, who use it to this day, have recourse, as I have already shown, to very moderate temperatures. For further corroboration of the argument, let us glance at the purpose of the bath —its intention is to *warm*, to *relax*, to induce a *gentle, continuous,* and *prolonged perspiration.* It is obvious that a gentle temperature will effect this object more thoroughly and completely than a burning, parching temperature of 150° and upwards. Our purpose is not to dry up the tissues, to rob the blood of its diluent fluid, but to soften the callous scarf-skin that it may be peeled off, and

to take away the excess of fluids pervading the economy, and with this excess any irritant and morbid
matters which they may hold in solution.

But all this while I have been infringing one of
the rules of the bath ; I have been talking in the
bath, and talking is of doubtful propriety ; the de-
meanour of the bather while in the bath must be
tranquil, composed, calm ; he must give himself up
to the dissolving process without exertion of muscle
or mind ; he may rub his skin gently ; he may talk
gently, sententiously, like a Turk, but he must not
allow himself to become animated, and above all,
he must not be vociferous.   The bath is a practice
intended for the body's health, and therefore deserves all our consideration and respect.   The rule
of Mr. Witt's bath cannot be too closely adhered to
—*only one talker at a time*—and it has the further
advantage that the talker knowing himself listened
to, takes time to think before he speaks.

In my experience it has rarely happened that a
novitiate has felt any inconvenience on his first entrance into the bath.   The practised bather is never
disturbed from the beginning to the end of the process.   But the beginner may, after the first quarter
of an hour, or when the perspiration is coming
forth in abundance, feel a little oppression, sometimes a little faintness, and sometimes a little increased action of the heart.   WHENEVER THIS IS
THE CASE HE SHOULD STEP OUT OF THE CALIDARIUM;
if there be a Tepidarium he will go into it, if not, he

may step into the Frigidarium. The uneasy feeling soon passes away, and then he should return to the Calidarium. He may do this as often as he likes, and with the most perfect safety; and *with this hint* it will be his own fault if he suffer any inconvenience whatever. The remedy is not so simple when, as sometimes happens, the fount of perspiration is as yet unopened, when the bather has never perspired, or to a very imperfect and trifling extent. Here, of course, the relief which is afforded to the system by perspiration is absent, and the bather may be seriously incommoded. He must not persist; force is antagonistic to the animal economy; he must succumb, and essay to bring about perspiration by the steady use of the vapour bath,—by such a bath, in fact, as the middle room of the Turkish bath. I know many persons who have never perspired, to whom the luxury of the bath is consequently lost. I know others who cannot perspire in dry air, but can do so in vapour. How frequently we are brought to reflect on the wisdom of the Turks, who have added so much vapour to their bath since they received it as an inheritance from the Romans.

How long shall I continue in the bath, says Amicus? —As long, my friend, as may be agreeable to yourself. You do not ask me how long you shall eat, nor how long you should sit at table. The instinct that tells you to place your knife and fork across your plate, must also direct you in finishing your bath. Something will depend, it is true, on the temperature, and the rapidity of the process of perspiration. If the temperature have been very agreeable, and perspiration slow, continuous, and efficient, you may pass the best part of an hour in the Calidarium. If it have been too hot, and the process untimely hurried, you must bring your enjoyment more speedily to an end.

We shall suppose that our friends have enjoyed their bath, and have agreeably spent three-quarters of an hour in the Calidarium :—the skin is now warm and moist, and the whole frame, its muscles and its joints, are softened and relaxed. This is the proper state and period, for those operations on the muscles and joints which are called SHAMPOOING. But as the art of shampooing is unknown in this country, or, if attempted, is practised only in the public baths, we must be contented in our private bath to pass over that process, the SECOND of the bath, and betake ourselves to that which follows, the *rolling* or *peeling* of the scarf-skin.

We cannot, however, wholly pass by the process of shampooing without a cursory glance at the nature of the operation and the manner of its performance. In the *inner room* of the Turkish bath, we have, following the description of Mr. Urquhart, seen the bather laid upon his back, on the marble platform under the centre of the dome, his mantle converted into a sheet to protect him from the heat of the marble, and his turban placed beneath his head in the guise of a pillow. The shampooer, or *tellak* as he is termed—and to perform the operation properly there should be two,—"kneels at your side, and bending over, grips and presses your chest, arms, and legs, passing from part to part, like a bird shifting its place on a perch. He brings his whole weight on you with a jerk, follows the line of muscle with anatomical thumb, draws the open hand strongly over the surface, particularly round the shoulder, turning you half up in so doing; stands with his feet on the thighs and on the chest, and slips down the ribs; then up again three times; and, lastly, doubling your arms one after the other on the chest, pushes with both hands down, beginning at the elbow, and then, putting an arm under the back and applying his chest to your crossed elbows, rolls on you across till you crack. You are now turned on your face, and, in addition to the operation above described he works his elbow round the edges of your shoulder-blade, and with the heel plies hard the angle of the neck; he concludes by hauling the body half up by each arm successively, while he stands with one foot on the opposite thigh. You are then raised for a moment to a sitting posture, and a contortion given to the small of the back with the knee, and a jerk to the neck by the two hands holding the temples."

At Dar el Baida Mr. Urquhart enjoyed the opportunity of "examining a public bath of the

Moors belonging to their good times. The disposition varies from that of the ancient Thermæ and
the modern Hamâms. The grand and noble portion of the Turkish and the ancient bath was a
dome, open to the heavens in the centre." Such a
dome, without the opening in the centre, exists in
the Moorish bath, but it is the inner and not the
outer apartment. "The vault has deep ribs in the
fashion of a clam shell, and is supported upon columns
with horse-shoe arches spreading between. Instead
of a system of flues through the walls, only one
passed through the centre under the floor. To get
at it, I had to break through the pavement of
beaten mortar covering a slab of marble. It was
nearly filled up with a deposit, partly of soot and
partly of earthy matter, which I imagined to be the
residuum of gazul." The examination of this bath
awakened a desire to experience the process of the
bath as practised among this ancient people. There
was a bath in the house of the Governor of the
province, but the Governor was away, and it was
not until Mr. Urquhart had sustained a long religious argument with the Caid, that he was permitted to complete his experience. His bath
attendant and shampooer was the sub-governor ;
and the occurrence was to be kept secret from the
inhabitants of the town on religious grounds. This
may explain, perhaps, the roughness of the reception
which Mr. Urquhart met with, and the absence of

,those refinements and comforts which commonly
belong to the Eastern bath.

The bather, he says, "enters the Calidarium
naked, he has no bath linen; the bath-room is
single, and placed over an oven; while a caldron
of water, heated on the fire below, throws its steam
into the apartment. The floor is burning hot; he
has no pattens; and boards are laid for him to
tread upon; the glove operation commences at
once. There was a dish of gazul for the shampooer
to rub his hands in. I was seated on the board with
my legs straight out before me; the shampooer
seated himself on the same board behind me, stretching out his legs. He then made me close my fingers
upon the toes of his feet, by which he got a pur-
chase against me, and rubbing his hands in the
gazul, commenced upon the middle of my back,
with a sharp motion up and down, between beating
and rubbing, his hands working in opposite directions. After rubbing in this way the back, he
pulled my arms through his own and through each
other, twisting me about in the most extraordinary
manner, and drawing his fingers across the region of
the diaphragm, so as to make me, a practised bather,
shriek. After rubbing in this way the skin, and
stretching at the same time the joints of my upper
body, he came and placed himself at my feet, deal-
ing with my legs in like manner. Then thrice
taking each leg and lifting it up, he placed his head

under the calf, and raising himself, scraped the leg
as with a rough brush, for his shaved head had the
grain downwards. The operation concluded by his
biting my heel."

The Moorish bath "certainly does clear off the
epidermis, work the flesh, excite the skin, set at
work the absorbent and exuding vessels, raise the
temperature, apply moisture ;—but the refinements
and luxuries are wanting."

Captain Clark Kennedy and his friends met with
no such difficulties as those experienced by Mr.
Urquhart.   After a fatiguing day's journey, they
visited a public Moorish bath at Medeah, and Captain Kennedy records their experiences, which
show a family resemblance to the Turkish Hamâm.
Passing, he says, "through a narrow passage, we
entered a room with two sides, occupied by a
sloping divan seven feet wide, and raised a couple
of feet from the floor."   "We took off our clothes,
replaced them with a voluminous wrapper of white
cotton, and thrusting our toes into leather loops
tacked to a pair of wooden soles, shuffled along, led
by an attendant, to a small apartment, full of steam
and tolerably warm, adjoining the bath-room.
Here we changed our drapery for dark cotton hand-
kerchiefs, fastened round the waist like kilts, and
passed on into a vaulted stone chamber, lit by a
solitary lamp hanging from the roof, whose sickly
light, struggling with the clouds of steam and the
darkness, just rendered visible the strange forms of

the bath attendants, naked, like ourselves, to the waist, with a single lock of dark hair, dripping with moisture, dangling from each uncovered shaven head.

" The pavement was flooded with hot water, and at first the heat was so oppressive I could hardly breathe; but the feeling went off after having been seated for a few minutes on a stone bench in the centre of the bath. We were now all laid out in a row on the pavement, each stretched on a blue cloth, with a rolled-up towel under the head, and an operator for each person. My attendant was a musical character, for when he commenced sham-pooing he accompanied his labours with a song, marking the chorus at the end of each verse by a punch of extra force. Being well soaked and softened, I was now scrubbed with a camel's-hair glove until I felt as if I had no skin at all. I then had my legs and arms pulled, my head screwed round with a jerk, was then doubled up like a boot-jack by his kneeling on my shoulders, my arms were brought behind me, and while his knee was forced into the hollow of my back, two or three dexterous twists put in motion each rib and ver-tebra; he then finished by endeavouring to crack, separately, every toe and finger. A large bowl of soap-suds was now brought, and, with a handful of the soft fibres of the aloe, he lathered me from head to foot. A plentiful supply of hot water was now poured over me, and, reconducted into the interior, I was enveloped in clean, white, warm linen, a long soft towel was wrapped round my head as a turban ; and, lastly, taken into the outer room, I was laid upon the divan with three or four sheets over all." " The feeling of lightness and elasticity given to a fatigued and stiffened body by a Moorish bath cannot be imagined without being felt." " It was too much trouble at the time to analyse my own feelings, but I remember the predominant idea was that I felt exceedingly comfortable." The process lasted two hours.

And now a word as to the operation of shampooing. Any inhabitant of a Northern climate like our own must read these descriptions of the process with wonder not unmixed with dread. Who but a professed acrobat would venture to submit to an operation in which a man "stands with his feet on the thighs and on the chest, and slips (his feet) down the ribs, then up again three times?" or "putting an arm under the back, and applying his chest to your crossed elbows, rolls on you across till you crack?" I have already explained that the operation of shampooing requires that the skin and the whole body, especially the muscular system, should be thoroughly softened before this process is commenced; and it would appear that when the proper degree of softening is attained, the Eastern people, who are remarkable for the pliability and elasticity of their joints, can support the operation without inconvenience. But the Northern races

are built for strength and endurance; their quality
is solidity, not pliability; their joints are too firmly
knit, and the bones too strongly braced together, to
permit of the application of such force as would
make the skeleton crack, without serious inconvenience and, indeed, danger. We have but to see
the Asiatic throw his foot over his shoulder, bend
his finger upon the back of his hand, crack every
joint of the fingers with the most moderate traction, or drop gracefully upon the ground, sitting on
the side of the foot, with the sole upturned towards
the skies, to be assured that there is something in
the structure of the bones and joints of the Asiatic
that does not exist amongst us. And if one of
these people were to tie himself up in a knot, we
should not be much surprised. We know, also, that
this curious pliability of the frame is enjoyed by
Europeans born and reared in the East ; and, moreover, that where it exists in a most perfect degree
while such persons are residing in the East, it is
considerably diminished, and even lost, on their
migration to a cold climate. There are, doubtless,
many persons amongst us who could bear the
Turkish process of shampooing, and particularly
after a sojourn of some time in the East, where the
climate alone would tend to soften their organism ;
and we can comprehend how a sailor, whose special
education is pliability and ductility of body and
limb, could go through the process creditably; but
we cannot realize the same of the soldier or the

ploughman; and as little should we tolerate a similar penance ourselves. Turkish shampooing may continue to be practised in the Turkish Hamâm, but the process must be considerably modified before it can become popular in Britain.

There can be no doubt that a modified shampooing would form a valuable addition to the Anglo-Turkish bath; that the friction of the skin, the pressing and kneading of the muscles, the traction of the sinews, the playing of the joints, even a certain pressure of the viscera, would be attended with benefit; and when there existed stiffening or thickening from chronic disease, as of rheumatism and gout, of immense advantage. The British shampooer has all this to learn, and we commend to him two considerations—agility and moderation.

After the shampooing—the second operation of the bath, that which immediately follows the seasoning of the body by warmth and moisture—there comes the THIRD OPERATION, the rolling and peeling of the outer layers of the scarf-skin; an operation in which the Turks are very expert. The scarf-skin has become softened and swollen by the warm moisture of the atmosphere and the exudation of perspiration from the skin, and is in a state ready for peeling and collecting into rolls and removing by the process of friction with the camel's-hair or goat-hair glove, the *kheesah* of India. In this operation there is no soap employed, the skin is as yet untouched with soap, and we rely for our success on simple friction. The Moors commence the process a little earlier, before the scarf-skin is thoroughly soaked, and use *gazul*. The Turks give a longer period to the softening of the albuminous layers of the epidermis, and *gazul* ceases to be necessary. We have no grease well powdered with dust to require the *strigil* of the Romans; we have no *gazul;* and we therefore follow in the footsteps of the Turk: we soak lengthily, lazily in our Tepidarium, or the cooler side of our Calidarium, and when we have artistically softened the epiderm, when we are done to a turn, we assume the glove, and we sweep with long strokes and firmly over the skin from the nuque to the podex, from the brow to the toe's end, until we have rolled and slid off the softened layers, and have developed the pure and satiny surface beneath. The old scarf is shed, we cast our exuviæ, and we are refulgent in the brightness and purity of our newest garment. After this, a warm flood of water, rushing upon us like a summer shower, or streaming over us like a waterfall from the regions of the sun; and all the foul scales that constitute the paved mosaic of the outward man are washed clean away.

In the public bath, this delicious operation is performed by the bath attendant, by the shampooer, the tellak, or in whatever other name he may delight. In the private bath, the host is so

condescending as to give his guest a rub down, or
an obliging and expert "companion of the bath"
does the kind office for his fellow C.B., particularly
if he be a callous, horny-skinned, and begrimed novitiate. We have seen Mr. Witt playing the camel's-
hair glove, with the grace of an Apollo, by the
hour; we have had our own epidermal integument
groomed with most exquisite tenderness by a noble
of the highest rank, for the time our "companion
of the bath;" by those veteran pioneers of the
bath, Mr. Witt and Mr. Rolland; and we have
travelled in imagination to the ancient Phœnician
city of Dar el Baida, nay, to the antediluvian
Baalbec itself, gazing in admiration on the very
features of the "giants that lived in those days,"
and on their marvellous achievements, and em-
barking with Noah and his sons in their vast and
wonderful ship, while Mr. Urquhart has been sweeping adown our back and limbs with the camel's-
hair pad filled with Mauritanian gazul, at his delightful Tusculum at Riverside.

The next operation, the FOURTH in order of proceeding, brings into play the soap and the wisp of
the white fibre of the Mecca palm—the *lyf*. The
bather stands before the operator, or sits on the
margin of the sunken basin that serves as a *lavatrina* or *labrum*; the operator draws towards him
the wooden basin, half filled with warm water, or
warm suds, or in the Turkish Hamâm with soft
soap; he dips his white bunch of lyf in the snowy

lather, or rubs it well with Castile or ordinary
soap, and he then gently, but thoroughly, glides
over the entire surface of the bather, from the
crown of the head to the soles of the feet. How
exquisite is the feeling of the cleansing operation
to the sensorium of the skin; and how still more
enjoyable is the warm cascade which bursts over
him as soon as the soaping and its accompanying
friction are at end; how difficult to bring the mind
to the belief that we have had enough. Were not
thankfulness in the ascendant at our recovered
purity, we might be so sinful as to regret that so
delicious an enjoyment had come to an end.

But if the sensation of the warm shower is
agreeable, no less so is the process which immediately succeeds—namely, a douse, or douche, of
the coldest water. The body is so thoroughly
warmed by the preceding operations, that instead
of striking a chill, as might be imagined by the
inexperienced, the coldness is most grateful, and
the feeling of freshness most exhilarating. Sometimes, an alternate douche of hot and cold water
is repeated in rapid succession, and it is a little
difficult for the bather to say which of the two is
at the moment bursting over him.

The intention of the cold affusion is to produce
contraction of the seven millions of pores which
open on the surface of the skin. They have acted
freely, they have performed the duty that was
required of them: the key may now be turned, the

lock closed ; they may be sealed up for the present, to be ready for further service at a future time. The Romans often concluded their bath by plunging into a cold pool, to attain the same object—the closure of the pores ; and the Turks, as we have already seen, omit the cold affusion, excepting to the feet, and rely upon the cool atmosphere of their great hall, open to the sky, and to the cooling influence of the current of air produced by a fan.

Where a middle room or Tepidarium exists, the process of washing, beginning with the inunction with soap and ending with the cold douche, is performed in that apartment. But where there is no Tepidarium, the process is gone through in some convenient part of the Calidarium. If the former, the bather returns to the Calidarium, and sits down for a few minutes, until the skin becomes warm, and any coldness is removed which may have been occasioned by the douche. Or, if the Calidarium have been the scene of the lavatory process, the bather, in like manner, takes his seat on a bench until all chill is dispelled.

With a skin perfectly warm, though no longer perspiring, the bather now steps out of the Calidarium, receiving either immediately before his exit, or as soon as he may have entered the Frigidarium, a warm, dry cotton mantle for his body, and a warm, dry napkin for his head ; the wet hip-cloth is left behind in the Calidarium, or is dropped at the entrance of the Frigidarium. The head and face are rubbed dry by means of the napkin, and the mantle or sheet is wrapped around the body and limbs, and the bather seats himself, or reclines on the couch of repose, according to his taste ; he remains passive, or calmly conversing, and awaits with patience the drying of his skin.

A good Frigidarium should be, as its name implies, as cool as possible ; a breeze of air sweeping through the room is an advantage ; the windows should be open, for the bather courts the cool air, and delights in feeling it play over his heated limbs. The Romans had an open terrace connected with the Frigidarium, in which the bathers could walk, enveloped in their mantle ; and a walk in the open air, or in one of the charming garden walks described by Pliny, would be most enjoyable. No wiping, no friction is necessary to dry the skin ; the mantle absorbs some, and the cool air dissipates the rest of the moisture. And after awhile the skin is left dry, satiny, and warm, without trace of moisture or clamminess, and in a state in which the usual dress may be resumed. This is the moment at which the description of Mr. Urquhart is properly applicable :—" The body has come forth shining like alabaster, fragrant as the cistus, sleek as satin, and soft as velvet."

The bather should now put on his clothing slowly and composedly ; no haste should hurry his movements, for haste might re-excite the perspiration, the skin might again become moist, and *then* there

would be danger of taking cold.   But if the process
be properly conducted, cold is impossible ; even the
sensation of cold is for the time lost.   The bather
feels renovated, restored, buoyant, good-tempered,
strong, the *beau idéal* of God's divinest creation—
man.

Let me illustrate the action of the bath by a
recent experience of my own, and at the same time
draw attention to the proper use of the bath, and
its singular power of effacing fatigue and painful
sensation of every kind—among others, the im-
perious craving of hunger.   A few weeks back,
after a day of severe labour, prolonged from six in
the morning until· after seven at night, I arrived
hungry and weary at the house of my friend, Mr.
Stewart Rolland.   I was expected, but was late ;
and, as I entered his library, dinner was being
served. " Will you sit down with us," was my host's
salutation, " or will you take a bath ?" " The bath !"
was my answer.   *" Ruat cœlum !"*

I had only to step into the next apartment, after
I had divested myself of my clothes, to find a
temperature of 150°.   I took my place on a couch
covered with a soft Turkish sheet, and was soon
covered with perspiration, first as a thick dew, and
then as a dripping shower.   The half-hour sand
glass had nearly run out, when I entered the
Lavatorium ; I soaped myself thoroughly from
crown to sole ; I turned a tap, when a cascade of
warm water poured over me, and rinsed away every

particle of soap ; a second tap, and I was in the midst of a sheet of cold water. The pores were now shut, and I returned to the Calidarium. A few minutes sufficed to warm the skin, and then, wrapped in a warm and dry mantle, I returned to the cooling room, and threw myself on a divan.

In twenty minutes I was dry and dressed, and in a state fitting to return to my friends, and eat with appetite and with the certainty of digestion, anything that might be set before me.

In the bath my fatigue had gone ; the craving hunger which I suffered on entering had ceased ; natural appetite had taken the place of morbid hunger ; the tired stomach had regained its power, and was in a fitting state not only to receive whatever food was given to it, but, better still, to digest it. No wonder that the Arab of the desert prefers the bath to food, and even to sleep ; it supplies the place of both.

I have portrayed Mr. Witt's bath ; let me endeavour to draw a sketch of Mr. Urquhart's bath —a bath dear to the memory of all early bathers —the bath at Riverside. We arrive at the door of the Frigidarium, we loosen the latchets of our shoes, and we leave them behind the lintel; the portal opens, and we enter. The apartment is small, but it is sunny and bright ; through the glass doors we see a balcony festooned with the tendrils of the rose, now leafless and out of bloom, for it is early winter; beyond the parapet of the balcony

are terraces of which the rose is still the favoured
ornament; further on, the rippled surface of a
boisterous, noisy stream; then meadows with
grazing herds and flocks, and the faithful horse;
beyond, the wooded hill, arching like an eyebrow
around the bright spot in which, as the apple of the
eye, sparkles the bath.   At our side is a dureta;
over against us a reclining chair; and along the
sides of the apartment a soft-cushioned divan; in
mid space a *sofra* supporting a nargillé; while
around are books, some Turkish ornaments and
chibouques; we tread on the carpet of Persia and
the clean, fresh, matting of India.   Opposite the
glass doors is an immense sheet of plate glass,
through it we see marble steps, and in the depths
to which these steps descend there is the reflection
of the sun.   Shades of Mecænas and Pliny, will ye
not smile?   Shade of Seneca, look not austere at
the luxury of this Briton of ancient descent; who
courts the rays of Phœbus, smiling through festoons
of roses, to visit the deepest pool of his bath.
Here he can swim, while the sun glistens in the
crystal drops that linger on his skin, or makes
mimic rainbows in the spray that he dashes before
him in his plunging revel.

A door opens by the side of the immense barrier
of glass; we enter; the door closes behind us.   Then
a second door; we pass through that, and we are
greeted with a delightful atmosphere; experience
tells us that no place of terrestrial existence can

yield that soft, balmy, warm æther but one—that one, the bath. We descend two steps, and reach a platform, all of whitest marble; we become sensible of an increase of warmth to the soles of our feet as we descend, and we are glad to find soft napkins spread on the lower steps to catch our footfall. Two steps more, and then another platform : the apartment expands at this point into a large square lofty hall, and the marble platform stretches from side to side the whole breadth of the hall. We are sensible, as we stand on this platform, that we have reached the tropical line of the bath, and that at no great depth beneath our feet must be the Hypocaust. To our right is a small square tent, surrounded with scarlet hangings; this is the *hottest of hots*, the Spartan Laconicum; it is placed immediately over the furnace. We glance within the parting curtains of the entrance; we see a cushioned divan of tempting softness. At a later stage of our bath, we pass ten minutes in that fiery tent; its customary temperature is 240° or 250°.

On the left of our present station is another divan, not enclosed by curtains like the other, but admitting of being so if required. On this divan, at a later stage of the bath, I spent many minutes of genuine enjoyment; being farther from the furnace, but still over the meridian of the Hypocaust, it was less hot than the enclosed tent: its common temperature is 170°. "If you would like a breath of fresh air," said my host, "draw out that plug."

G

I saw a plug just above my head, just near enough
to reach by stretching out my hand. I withdrew
it, not because I wanted air, but in a spirit of
obedience, or, if you will, of lazy indolence. What
a reward! what a delicious gush of ambrosial air!
Heavens! what Sybaritic contrivance is here? I
looked round for the shade of old Pliny, expecting
to see him peering over my shoulder; but he was
not there; the modest Roman shade was abashed,
was vanquished by the modern Mecænas: the perfume was that of mignionette! Although the last
of the season, enough remained to enable my fancy
to judge how delicious that air must have been a
month or two earlier. This was one of the venti-
lating-holes of the bath, and my host had brought
the air that was to cool his bath from the perfumed
atmosphere of a bed of mignionette. How I longed
at that moment for one half-hour of summer, that
I might test the other spiracles, that I might perchance inhale the breath of roses here, and violets
or lilies there.

And now comes a deeper descent (four steps),
and behold, I am on the floor of the bath. Still
costly marble greets my tread. In the corner opposite the fiery tent is another divan; here, far removed from the torrid meridian, the temperature is
still lower (about 150°), but the atmosphere is everywhere fresh: it is clear that ventilation is perfect,
and there are no vapoury mists, no fleeting gauze of
ghost-like moisture.

I am permitted to gaze about me for a while, when my host leads me to a small recess on the side corresponding with the couch of perfume. A curtain is withdrawn, and I perceive that the bottom of this recess is below the level of the floor, and that a marble step placed at one end breaks the descent to the bottom. The bottom, also, is peculiar: the marble slab slopes downwards to an opening, through which water finds its way into the drain. I am aware that this is the Lavaterina or Latrina—that here the novitiate is made to pass through the first ordeal of the bath. Before he entered the sacred precincts of the Apodyterium, he undid the latchets of his shoes : he left his shoes beyond the door ; he brought with him none of the dust of the external world into the portals of the bath. In the Frigidarium, or rather in the Apodyterium, he left behind him his vestments, and assumed the simple garb of the inner bath. Now, and before he can claim to select his place on the divans, he pays a further tribute to the god of purity: the outer layers of his scarf-skin must be peeled away—he must yield up his skin to the ordeal of the glove, the *gazul*, or the soap; and then, semi-purified, he may range at will the apartment—he may explore at leisure the mysteries of the bath.

We seat ourselves on the clean marble at the edge of the Lavaterina ; our host plays the soft pad of *gazul* over the head, the back, the sides; we complete the operation on the limbs and feet ourselves ;

Basin after basin of warm water rinses the *gazul*
and the loosened epidermis from the surface, and
we rise from the Lavaterina to recommence our
observations.

Immediately in front of the flight of steps already
described, and occupying the centre of the remaining
wall of the hall, is a square pool, between four and
five feet in depth, and reached by several steps. In
this pool are two feet of water, perfectly cold, with
a tap from which as much may be obtained as may
be required. This water is pumped up from the
river, and filtered before it is admitted into the
bath: it, like the bather, is made to leave its dusty
shoes outside the door, and is thoroughly cleansed
before it is permitted to invade the sanctuary. In
this pool, this *piscina*, the bather refreshes himself with a plunge in cold water—in the summer
cooled down with ice—when he issues heated from
the "hottest of hots," or when he completes the
bath; and here he may take his dip or his plunge,
his douche or his swim, with the sun shining in
upon his polished skin.

Having received my freedom of the bath in the
Lavaterina, I commenced a series of visits to all the
soft, the warm, the perfumed, the hot, the cool, the
cold nooks, that I could find. I rolled in enjoyment
on the divan by the side of the *piscina*, watching
my "companions of the bath," and especially a little
Antinous, or rather an infant Hercules, of five
years of age, who one while crept into the fiery

tent, and another while disported himself like a
young sea-god, with evident delight, in the cold
piscina. I then took my place in the higher temperature of the torrid zone, on the divan that was
breathed over by the sweet expirations of the mignionette; and anon crept into the tent with the
scarlet curtains serving as a door, and wondered
that I could breathe an atmosphere heated to 240°
without inconvenience.

It was now approaching the hour of breakfast,
and however disinclined I might be to leave the
warm world in which I had spent more than an
hour, I was ready to acknowledge certain material
warnings of the charms of breakfast. Before, however, I could quit the bath, it was necessary that
the pores, which had been all this while filtering
the waste fluids of the body through their number-
less apertures, should be made to close ; and with
this intent I descended into the pool, to experience
and enjoy a new sensation. I crouched under the
tap, while a cold torrent poured over me, the little
Hercules catching greedily on his head any waste
jets that glanced aside, and then shaking his flaxen
ringlets over his face and shoulders with a joyous
laugh. But my last experience was to come. At
the word " Hold firm !" a full pail of hot water
rushed upon me like an avalanche, and was instantly
followed by the same quantity of cold; this was
repeated in quick succession a number of times, and
then, when my host's arms seemed tired of the

further repetition, I arose from the pool, and shook my soused frame on the platform above, with a feeling of freshness and vigour that I shall long remember—remember when the bath and all its vagaries shall have become too familiar to suggest a note of their early impressions.

I was soon warm enough to quit the region of water, and ascend into that of air—to quit the region of fire, and mount into that of the sun, then smiling beamingly in at the window. My host gave my head a good rub with a warm, soft Turkish napkin, and threw a warm mantle over my shoulders; and it was with a feeling of " divided duty," the bath on one side and the breakfast on the other, that I ascended to the Frigidarium. Throwing myself on a softly-cushioned dureta, a half-hour was spent in suggestive and instructive conversation, and then " to breakfast with what appetite we may." Shades of immortal Shakespeare ! Speaking for myself, I should say, with the appetite of a man. Need I say more. This is my memory of the delicious bath at Riverside.

My host placed before me a dish, or rather a basket, of that wonderful Moorish food, the *kuscoussoo*, and our conversation naturally drifted away to the mode of preparing food pursued by different nations, and particularly to the mode of its preparation in the countries where the particular food is indigenous. I was struck with my host's remark, that while we draw food from other countries, we fail to learn the native manner of preparing that food ; and that from our ignorance on this point we frequently deteriorate, and often destroy its properties altogether.

It is to be regretted that the very highest branch of the science of chemistry—that which has for its object the *preparation of the food* which God in his goodness has bestowed upon us, for the sustenance and preservation of His greatest work, man himself—should be so miserably neglected. How much happier man's state would be if this department of chemistry were more cultivated and better understood ; how greatly would the nutritive power of food be developed, how much would be economized in its use ! How much might even the life of man be prolonged ! Of the many that die daily in their beds, surrounded by warm coverings, costly hangings, and sorrowing friends, there are many who die of absolute starvation—starved, because the modern science of culinary chemistry has no better nourishment to offer than abominable beef-tea, wretched mutton-broth, miserable arrowroot or sago, or detestable gruel. Tell me, ye sick who have so narrowly escaped death, whether what I am saying is not perfectly true ; and that between nauseating physic on the one hand, and equally nauseating diet on the other, have you not " run the gauntlet" of destruction, from which your escape is indeed miraculous ?

The plan of the bath at Riverside was not lost upon me in an undertaking on which I was then engaged—namely, building a bath for myself. My Apodyterium is at the back of my house; from this a Xystos, with a glazed roof, leads to the outer door of the Calidarium. Within the outer door is a vestibule, which upon occasion may serve as a Tepidarium. At the end of the vestibule is a second door, and this opened, we are in the Calidarium, an apartment more than ten feet high, fifteen feet long, and twelve wide. Along the side of the room runs a flue, with an area of four feet by nine inches; the flue crosses the end, and returns for a distance of two feet on the opposite side. At the point of return is the chimney. Two windows with thick glass let light into the room; and five circular openings, four inches in diameter, and closed by a telescopic lid (Looker's ventilator), supply an abundance of air; while a similar ventilator in the chimney-shaft secures its free circulation. The floor is a tesselated pavement of coloured octagonal tiles; and on the side corresponding with the door is a sunken Lavaterina, three feet six in length, two in breadth, and eighteen inches deep. Over the centre of the Lavaterina are two spouts, for cold and hot water; the latter being obtained from a galvanized iron tank, capable of holding twenty-five gallons, that stands on the returned flue, against the chimney-shaft. In this bath, as in Mr. Urquhart's, I expect to get various degrees of temperature, increasing in altitude from a temperate standard in the vestibule, to the highest temperature that can be required, immediately over the furnace, where I have established my Laconicum.

CHAPTER II.*

REVIVAL AND SANITARY PURPOSES OF THE EASTERN BATH.

THE Eastern Bath in its essential nature is a well ventilated apartment, in which the air is heated to an average temperature of 130 degrees of Fahrenheit. The bather sits, or reclines, or stands, in this apartment, moving about at his pleasure; while the heat, by its stimulant action on the skin, causes the perspiration to issue from its seven millions of pores, and to flow over the surface in greater or less abundance. While the perspiration is spreading in a sheet over the skin, trickling downwards in lively rills, and falling in continuous drops from all the salient points of the frame, the bather gently rubs his body and limbs with his hands; the softened cuticle is raised in thin flakes, and if the bath be taken but seldom, the cuticle is rubbed up in such quantity as to form little elliptical rolls, more or less begrimed with dirt. After the lapse

---

* This chapter is an abstract of a Paper read at the meeting of the National Association for the Promotion of Social Science, in Glasgow, in Sept. 1860.

of a certain number of minutes, varying from twenty to sixty or more, the bather soaps himself thoroughly; he then receives a shower of warm water, which washes the soap and impurity from the surface, and is most agreeable to the sensations. He next has a shower or douche of cold water, which effects the closure of the gaping pores, and is extremely refreshing. He then envelopes his body in a cotton mantle or sheet, and retiring to a cool room, to which the external air is freely admitted, he sits or reclines, remaining as impassive as possible, until the skin is thoroughly dried, and feels smooth and satiny in every part. The bather then resumes his usual dress, and the process is complete.

THE SANITARY PURPOSES which the bath is calculated to fulfil are three in number, namely:—

1. PRESERVATION OF HEALTH.
2. PREVENTION OF DISEASE.
3. CURE OF DISEASE.

The bath is *preservative of health,* by maintaining a vigorous condition of the body; a state the best suited for the happiness of the individual, as rendering him in the highest degree susceptible of the enjoyment of life; and a state the most advantageous to social interests, as ensuring the highest working condition.

The bath is *preventive of disease,* by hardening the individual against the effects of variations and vicissitudes of temperature, by giving him power to resist miasmatic and zymotic affections, and by

strengthening his system against aberrations of
nutrition and the fecund train of ills that follow
disturbance of the nutritive functions—namely,
scrofula, consumption, gout, rheumatism ; diseases
of the digestive organs ; cutaneous system ; muscular
system, including the heart ; nervous system, including the brain ; and reproductive system.

The bath is *a cure for disease* when the latter
state is already established, and is a powerful and
effective medicine.

These are a general summary of the nature and
attributes of the Eastern bath, which I shall now
endeavour to illustrate with more exactness and in
greater detail.

It is an interesting and important feature in
connexion with the revival of the bath in Britain,
after a lapse of fifteen hundred years, that it should
have been so eagerly taken up and adopted by the
working classes.   Several baths, founded and maintained by working men, have been established in
our great manufacturing towns—among others, in
Bradford, Barnsley, Sheffield, Manchester, Leeds,
Staleybridge, Rotherham, and Rochdale ; and this
fact, together with the general popularity of the
bath among the artisan class, will doubtless lead
the thinking man to recognise in the institution
attributes of sterling value and prospective public
utility.

The processes which constitute the Eastern bath
—in other words, the stages of the bath—are three
in number, namely :—1. Exposure of the naked
body to hot dry air ; 2. Ablution with warm and
cold water; and, 3. Cooling and drying of the
skin.—The bath, or thermæ, should therefore con-
sist of three apartments devoted especially to the
three processes—namely, the hot room, or Calidarium ; the washing room, or Lavatorium; and the
cooling room, or Frigidarium. Or, for private use,
two rooms; or one room divided into two compartments, Calidarium and Frigidarium, would be
sufficient; the Calidarium being used as a Lavato- ·
rium after the sweating process is completed.

My friend, Mr. George Witt, of Prince's Terrace,
Hyde Park, to whom I am indebted for my first
introduction to the bath, possesses a bath of the
simple construction to which I am now alluding;
and as it fulfils very satisfactorily all the purposes
of the bath, I shall proceed to describe it, by way
of illustration of one of the simplest forms of bath
for private use. On the ground-floor of his house
he had a room twenty feet long by ten feet in
breadth, and twelve feet high, with a window looking out upon a lead flat. To convert this room
into a thermæ he divided it into two compartments, by means of a wall which crossed it at
about one-third from its further end. He had thus

two apartments—an outer one, the Frigidarium; and an inner one, entered by two small doors, outer and inner, in the partition wall, the Calidarium. To preserve the heat of the Calidarium a lath and plaster lining was placed inside and at the distance of a few inches from the wall, and the space between the lining and the wall filled in with sawdust. The same was done to the ceiling, and the floor was paved with earthen tiles set on concrete. On the side corresponding with the exterior of the house a square of thick glass was let into the wall, and, above and below, were four circular holes three inches in diameter, and fitted with plugs for the purpose of ventilation. Further, in the partition wall was a small square of glass through which a thermometer could be seen from the outside, and a gas-burner from the inside, enabling the bather to ascertain the temperature of the Calidarium from the outside without opening the doors, and supplying a light exterior to the Calidarium when the bath is used in the evening.

Following this description, it will be seen that the Calidarium or Sudatorium is simply a closed chamber, with an area of sixty-five superficial feet, and containing seven hundred and fifteen cubic feet of atmospheric air, the actual measurements being ten feet long by six feet and a half wide, and eleven feet high; this chamber being provided with sufficient means of ventilation through the agency of the imperfectly-fitting doors, and also the occasional opening of the doors on one side, and the four holes, already described as existing in the exterior wall, on the other; and also, supposing the doors to be more closely shut, between an ingoing current of cold air through the two lower holes, and an outgoing current of hot air through the upper holes. Ten persons can take the bath without discomfort, and without being overcrowded in Mr. Witt's thermæ; I have myself formed one of nine, but with six or seven the space is more than ample.

Let me now turn to the means of heating the Calidarium. In the exterior wall, near its bottom, and opening on the lead flat, is a furnace of the commonest possible construction, and capable, from its free draught, of burning the commonest combustible material—such as inferior coal, coal screenings, coke, cinders, and sawdust. This furnace, encased in brickwork, is carried obliquely for a distance of four or five feet into the Calidarium; and its flue, following the angle of the floor, makes the circuit of the apartment. The flue next ascends perpendicularly for a few feet, crosses the wall above the brickwork which encloses the furnace, and then makes its way up the angle of the room to the ceiling, where it escapes by means of a chimney. The flue, in its course around the room, is raised from the level of the floor, and separated from the wall by the breadth of a brick, and consequently presents a free surface on all sides for the radiation of heat. Its radiating surface is about

one foot square, and its length thirty-five feet. The
common temperature maintained in Mr. Witt's
Calidarium is 130° to 140° of Fahrenheit. Mr.
Witt tells me that he has had it as high as 180°;
and I have myself been in it, in company with my
friend Mr. Chadwick, at 150° of Fahrenheit.

As the British thermæ is at present in a state of
infancy, the question of construction, in reference
to the threefold condition, of size of apartment,
degree of ventilation and temperature, and materials, is before us for inquiry and research. The
common plaster walls of Mr. Witt's Calidarium
answer perfectly : they are not too hot for the
naked skin, as a glazed or polished material would
be ; and they admit of cleansing by water, whenever
necessary. The red and blue earthen tiles of his
bath give a pleasant holding to the soles of the
feet on account of their roughness, and with the
intramural position of the flue never become too
hot. Glazed tiles, although more elegant in appearance, are too hot for contact with the skin, and
require, consequently, to be trodden on with wooden
clogs; moreover, when at all moistened, they are
slippery and dangerous. Therefore, so far as our
present means of information go, it would appear
that the more economical materials of construction
answer in every way the best. We are, however,
still open to instruction on these points, as well as
in many others appertaining to the bath, and we
shall probably be doing best to adhere as closely as

possible to the Turkish model. Can the furnace, as at present described, be improved? What combustible material would be the most economical; taking into consideration the questions of price, of rapidity of combustion and of deposition of soot in the flue, requiring more or less frequent cleansing?

The flue in Mr. Witt's bath is constructed of galvanized iron plate, and is square in form. This flue answers very well, but Mr. Witt does not approve of iron, because in a hot dry atmosphere particles of the metal are thrown off and mingle with the air. The best material for the construction of the flue is earthen tiles or bricks; probably pipes fitting end to end may, with some modification, be made to answer the purpose, but heretofore they have been found to split with the heat. Then, in the case of building a bath, the relative value of bricks, and especially of hollow bricks, and pierced bricks, and bricks with a surface finish, come under consideration.

Immediately over the flue passing around the floor of the Calidarium is a wooden seat; and over the masonry of the furnace, a wooden step and platform affording additional sitting room. On the platform is a wooden couch, shaped like a straddling letter W, called the *dureta* from the hardness of its material, but in reality forming a most pleasant and agreeable couch, as the angles of the couch correspond with the joints of the body when in a reclining position. The dureta was borrowed by the Emperor Augustus from Spain, or rather from Morocco through Spain,* and contributes greatly to the luxury of the bath.

It is a fault in Mr. Witt's bath that the flue entirely surrounds the floor of the Calidarium, and consequently crosses the entrance door, rendering it necessary to the bather to step down from the seat to the floor of the apartment in going in, and to step upwards in going out. This arrangement leads to occasional slips, particularly when the floor is wet; and although unimportant to persons in the full vigour of health, calls for caution in all, and especially on the part of those who are in any degree infirm; and becomes a serious impediment where it is necessary to lift an invalid into the bath. Fortunately the inconvenience admits of an easy remedy; the flue, when it reaches the jamb of the doorway, may be carried over the door and so onwards along the side of the room; or it may be doubled back upon itself and made to return to the line from which it started, and then carried to any point of exit that may be suitable. A better material for the flue is brickwork; and as the intention of the flue is to afford a large surface for the radiation of heat, the plan has been adopted of making flues of large size, for example, three or four feet in height. A short length of a flue of these dimensions is equivalent to three or four times the length of a flue of one foot square, and its course

* "Pillars of Hercules."

along two or three sides of the room affords as much heat as can be required. I visited lately a small bath in Bell-street, Edgeware-road, in which a flue of this construction, about three feet in height and nine inches in width, ran along three sides of the room, and gave out a temperature of 160°.

In the Turkish bath and in some of the modern British Thermæ the flues are carried under the floor, constituting a kind of Roman *Hypocaustum*, and are made to describe a series of parallel rows, which traverse from side to side and are connected at the ends. A very high degree of temperature is attained by this arrangement, as in the private bath of Mr. Stewart Rolland, of Victoria-street, Westminster; but it presents this manifest objection, namely, that the floor is so hot as to be unbearable to naked feet or to a naked skin, and is therefore not without danger to an invalid who may have accidentally fallen on the ground. Again, where very high temperatures are obtained, the woodwork of the seats becomes so hot as to render coverings of some kind necessary. The temperature of Mr. Stewart Rolland's Calidarium, when fully heated, ranges between 150° and 170°, while with the aid of a *Laconicum* he is able to carry his temperature twenty degrees higher; his couches and seats are, therefore, covered with cotton sheets having a thick pile; and in place of wood he uses fibrous slabs, which have a lower conducting power and are less influenced by the heat. Moreover, in the construction of his walls he employs felt, on account of its non-conducting and non-inflammable properties, as an intermediate layer, in place of the sawdust used by Mr. Witt.

From want of space, as I have before remarked, Mr. Witt's Calidarium becomes his Lavatorium at the conclusion of the sweating process; and no inconvenience results from this arrangement, because ample time can be spared for the drying up of the moisture before the bath is required for use a second time. But where the requisite extent of space exists, and, as a necessity in a public bath where a succession of bathers enter and depart, a separate apartment should be devoted to the purposes of a Lavatorium. And, as the Lavatorium should adjoin the Calidarium, a few feet of the flue may be introduced into the partition wall between the two, and made to warm the air of the Lavatorium, converting it, in fact, into a Tepidarium. The Tepidarium of the ancient Roman Thermæ was an apartment of an intermediate temperature between the Frigidarium and the Calidarium, and supplied a transition medium between the two extremes; warming and relaxing the body on its way from the Frigidarium to the Calidarium on the one hand, and qualifying the depression of the temperature from the Calidarium to the Frigidarium on the other.

Before its escape from the Calidarium, the flue is made to heat the water which is required for rinsing the body after thorough friction with soap. For this purpose a tank holding a few gallons of water (Mr. Witt's tank holds ten gallons) is fixed on a portion of the flue at the upper part of the bath, and a short descending pipe, with a horizontal arm fitted at the end with a rose, distributes a grateful shower of warm water over the bather. Another horizontal arm, with or without a rose, brings the cold water, with which the ablution is completed, into the Lavatorium, and is distributed either as a copious shower or as a descending douche, as the bather may desire. In Mr. Stewart Rolland's bath I was indulged with an alternate douche of hot and cold water, which was wonderfully delicious.

The third compartment of the bath (the Frigidarium) may be as large as convenient, but should be abundantly supplied with the means of procuring fresh air, and even a current of air; it is not only a cooling-room, but also a drying-room, for in it the moisture left on the body is thoroughly evaporated, and the skin becomes smooth and satiny. The Frigidarium should be furnished with a couch and a few easy chairs, and as it is intended to be trodden with naked feet, it should have a clean wooden floor or a mat. Moreover, it is here that fresh water may be kept for drinking, or the acidulated drinks, or the sherbet. It is here also that should be found the *Columbarium*, with its pigeon-holes for receiving the mantles, the sheets, the towels, the cummer-

bunds, the combs, together with any other appur-
tenances of the bath that may be in use.

Again, in the two or three-roomed bath, a portion
of the Frigidarium may be devoted to the purpose
of a dressing-room, Apodyterium, or *Vestiarium.*
Here the clothes may be hung up on pegs as they
are removed, and here shoes and boots should be
left, the presence of shoes being strictly prohibited
in the proper cooling part of the room. In this
arrangement we are made aware that among the
Romans the Frigidarium and the Vestiarium were
separate apartments, and formed a portion of that
series which Pliny conceived might, with the
strictest economy of space, be comprehended in five
or seven rooms, but would be more completely
carried out in nine. The Frigidarium of the
Romans, like the Mustaby of the Turks, was open
to the vault of heaven.

Such is the Eastern bath, in reference to the
question of construction; it is either a spare room
with a partition, a furnace and chimney, and a small
reservoir of water; or it is an outhouse with a
similar arrangement; or it is five walls, with a
roof, erected in a convenient spot; or it is an
elegant "hothouse," pendent to a country villa; or
it may be an architectural wonder of ancient Roman
grandeur. In other words, it may come within the
reach of the poor man, at the expenditure of a few
shillings or pounds, or it may be the metamorphosis
of hundreds and thousands of pounds into a palace

of magnificence and luxury. But the poor man's bath will be essentially as perfect as that of Dives, and he will, if he be wise, carry the balance of cost to the education of his children. In a small society of neighbours, clubbing their means, the bath would cost less than the tobacco-pipe; and where the rules of the Bath are rigidly enforced, as they invariably should be, the Bath would become a school of moral discipline as well as physical health, and be a potent counterblast to the public-house.

OPERATION OF THE BATH.

We will now *take* a bath. We will endeavour to solve the question, WHAT IS THE BATH? We enter the Apodyterium or Vestiarium; we divest our body of its clothing; we hang our garments orderly on the apportioned pegs; we place our boots on the ground under our clothing, pushing the socks into the boots; we fold the *cummerbund*, a scarf of the Turkish red twilled cotton eight feet long and eighteen inches broad, around our hips, or we may prefer a kilt of the same material, or a pair of short drawers, and we are ready to enter the Tepidarium, if such there be; or, in the absence of a Tepidarium, the Calidarium. This is the costume of the Bath, and a costume is indispensable. Without a costume in the presence of others, the bath is not the bath—it is an evil, and as an evil it should be suppressed with the utmost severity. But I am not describing the Bath for those who would abuse it, but for those only who have the intelligence to apply it to the high and noble purposes of which it is capable. An addition to the above simple costume is sometimes made by folding a cotton scarf around the head—a kind of turban; and the turban has its advantages, as a protection of the bare head against the extreme heat of the apartment. The turban, when used by the gentler sex, protects and supports the hair, and the cummerbund gives place to a loose cotton chemise, that of the Turkish red twill being the most becoming and appropriate.

We now enter the Calidarium; we are impressed with the sensation of a most agreeable warmth; we look at the thermometer, we find the temperature to be 135° of Fahrenheit; we take our position on one of the seats, or we ascend upon the platform above, and we discover that a hard wooden couch, the *dureta*, may be the pleasantest couch in the universe. We look around us; the atmosphere is clear, there is no haze upon the window, the floor, the seats, and the walls are dry, and yet there is no oppression to the breathing organs; we breathe as agreeably as in the open air —nay, those who are ordinarily oppressed in the air from chronic bronchitis or asthma breathe more lightly and pleasantly here. But I must explain: I am now describing the sensations experienced in Mr. Witt's bath, and the freshness of the atmosphere of Mr. Witt's bath has always been praised by the most experienced bathers, and by those who have been accustomed to the Bath in the East. Mr. Witt attributes this virtue of his bath, and with apparent reason, partly to sufficient ventilation, and partly to the presence of his warm-water tank in the upper portion of the apartment; the water of this tank, evaporated by the heat of the flue, descends into the apartment, and pervades the atmosphere as an invisible vapour—a vapour which is felt, but not seen; and he further remarks that a similar effect is not attainable by the introduction of water on the floor of the bath.

If, after our first entrance into the Calidarium, we place the hand on any part of our skin, it gives the sensation of coldness, as compared with the temperature of the apartment. Soon, however, the skin becomes warm and dry; shortly afterwards it is moist and clammy; and later still, the perspiration begins to flow with greater or less activity. The freedom of perspiration follows the known structure of the skin in reference to the sudatory organs; it is first perceptible and most abundant on the face and hands, where the sudatory glands are most numerous and most developed; it succeeds on the chest and shoulders, then on the rest of the body, and lastly, on the legs below the knees. The perspiration at first issues from the pores in minute drops, the drops swell to the size of peas, and the skin looks as if it were garnished with crystal beads; the beads run into little rills, and the rills trickle down the hollow ways of the

surface in small streams.   It is at this period that
the whole body admits of being washed by means
of the water that issues from itself, and that the
secret of the small quantity of water provided for
the baths by the Romans is discovered.

It is when the perspiration commences to flow
in abundance, that the beginner in the use of the
bath, or the owner of a susceptible constitution,
becomes aware of an increase of rapidity of the
heart's pulsations ; and this sensation is commonly
associated with a feeling of oppression, something
approaching to faintness.   On the first hint of this
sensation, the bather should retire to the Tepidarium or to the Frigidarium, and sit there for a
few minutes, or until the sensation has ceased ; he
may then return to the Calidarium, and upon each
recurrence of the sense of oppression always quit
the Calidarium for the cooler temperature without.
The sensation which I am now describing is the
only disagreeable one attendant upon the use of the
bath ; it is unknown to the practised bather, and
to the strong or callous constitution, and may be
effectually obviated, even in the most sensitive, by
the simple precaution which I have just suggested.
Strange to say, these passages from the hot to the
cold temperature are not attended with a check to
the perspiration, they only moderate it, while the
stimulus of the fresh air provides more ample chest-
room for the oxygenization of the lungs.

One of the most curious, and at the same time

impressive, of the phenomena of the bath, is the relative freedom of perspiration of the educated and the uneducated skin; in other words, of the practised and the unpractised bather. There are certain persons who have never perspired, and these persons require a long training in lower temperatures before they can be admitted with safety to the higher temperatures; they are also much assisted by the addition of watery vapour to the hot air, converting it, in fact, into a vapour-bath. But of the rest of mankind, who present every facility for active perspiration, but who have never had, or but seldom have, the skin aroused to its normal activity, the variety in the energy of perspiration is very remarkable. The practised bather is enveloped in a sheet of perspiration, while the skin of the beginner is hardly moist; if the practised bather but raise his arm, the water drips from his elbows and finger-ends in continuous drops; his cummerbund is saturated, and the water may be wrung from it as from a soddened cloth, while the cummerbund of the neophyte is still dry. If the beginner rest his back for an instant against the wall of the Calidarium, he shrinks away from it, because of the intensity of its heat; but the practised bather presses against it with all his force, and receives only the sensation of an agreeable warmth, because the abundant moisture of his skin is sufficient to keep the wall cool. The beginner loses the moisture only of the surface of the body, and feels no resulting internal sensation;

but, in the practised bather, the skin sucks up the
watery fluids from the deeper streams of the san-
guine flood, and the bather thirsts in the operation.
He drinks water from time to time to replenish the
waste; pint upon pint is taken into his stomach,
and finds its way firstly into the blood, and then
into the sudatory system of the skin; surely an
apparatus of organs and a current of blood so
rinsed by the transit of pure water must undergo
an important purification. To the practised bather
the drinking of water during the perspiration of
the body is reviving and necessary, because his
blood has need of water to supply the place of that
which has been withdrawn by the skin, and the
amount of need is expressed by his thirst. But the
beginner has no thirst, and he will do well to avoid
drinking, as calculated to increase the labour of
perspiration, and likely therefore to be followed by
oppression and faintness.

The time passed in the Calidarium, with the
occasional retirements already mentioned, may vary
between twenty minutes and an hour; *a continuous
moderate perspiration of a certain duration* being
the object which should be kept in view. Besides
causing an active perspiration, the warmth and
moisture of the Bath soften the epiderm or scarf-
skin, and by gentle friction with the hand the
softened epiderm is rubbed off in small elliptical
cylinders. At the conclusion of the bath the skin
should be gently rubbed over with soap, applied

either with the kheesah or goat-hair glove, or with
a wisp of lyf—the white woody fibre of the Mecca
palm, commonly used for the purpose in the East.
After the friction with soap, the body should be
thoroughly rinsed by means of the warm shower-
bath ; and after the warm shower-bath follows a
shower of cold water, or a cold douche.   The idea
of a douse of cold water upon a fully perspiring
skin suggests a feeling of alarm in the minds of
those who have not experienced it, or have not
thought upon the matter ; but in practice it is
inexpressibly grateful to the sensations, and wholly
free from the shadow of danger.

The purpose of the cold douche is to cause a
sudden shrinking or contraction of the skin, and
this contraction closes all the pores, and tightens
and braces the cutaneous vessels.   The process is
necessarily accompanied with a trifling amount of
cooling of the surface, and the bather remains in
the Calidarium for a few minutes longer, until this
coolness has passed away, and the skin is everywhere
warm to the touch.   He then leaves the Calidarium,
and enters the Frigidarium.   When the bather
possesses a separate Lavatorium, the process of
soaping, with the subsequent ablutions, is performed
in that apartment ; and, being accomplished, he
returns to the Calidarium to recover his warmth,
and is then ready for the Frigidarium.   The warming of the body after the cold douche is thus shown
to be an important part of the bath—as, in fact, is

every process, howsoever trivial each may seem when considered separately and by itself.

On entering the Frigidarium the bather is enveloped in a large cotton sheet or mantle, which covers him from the head to below the feet ; he lies or sits down, enclosing each limb in a separate fold of the sheet, and he wipes his face and head with a dry napkin, or with a corner of the sheet. He then remains perfectly tranquil and quiescent, the sheet absorbs any excess of moisture, and the accumulated heat of the body disperses the rest. After fifteen or twenty minutes he exposes an arm to the air ; then both arms and the upper part of the trunk of the body; then the lower limbs; bringing every part of the skin in succession into relation with the cool air or cool breeze of the apartment. Of course, where an attendant is attached to the bath, the investiture with the mantle, the wiping of the head and face, the wrapping of the separate limbs, and the packing of the body, are performed by such attendant, or one bather performs the office for another ; but where the bather is alone, he finds no difficulty in doing it all for himself.

The cooling and drying process, which is the special use of the Frigidarium, is regarded by experts as not the least important part of the curriculum of the bath. It is here that the moisture is dissipated from the skin by the heat of the body, that the bather recovers from any little physical exhaustion that the processes of the Lavatorium may have occasioned, that the skin is brought into contact with the open air, and imbibes its oxygen ; that the man becomes sensible of a delicious repose of the nervous system, and an equally agreeable restoration of his powers. If the quiet impassibility of the Roman, or the listlessness of the Turk, is to be imitated in the preceding stages of the bath, it is doubly deserving of imitation here ; calm, repose, dignity, thankfulness, should fill the soul of the bather while in the Frigidarium. When his skin is perfectly dry, but still warm, smooth, and satiny to the touch, then, and then only; slowly and leisurely, he should begin to resume his usual clothing. If he dress too soon he will be apt to break out into a perspiration while putting on his clothes, or after quitting the bath ; in which case he will be in danger of taking cold, and frustrating the benefits of the bath.

SANITARY PURPOSES OF THE BATH.

In reference to the sanitary purposes of the bath, I assume that it is Preservative of Health ; that it is Preventive of Disease ; and that it is also Curative of Disease.

The mode in which its power operates in the fulfilment of these results is by the production and maintenance of a healthy skin. A healthy skin I therefore assume to be the end and aim of the bath ; and to support my argument it will be necessary that I should point out the importance

of a healthy skin in the animal economy, and those
conditions and circumstances of common life that
tend to deteriorate its structure and function; to
show, in fact, why the skin is worth preserving,
and how its preservation in a state of health con-·
duces to the health of the entire organism.

The skin, from its large extent, deserves to be
ranked among the great organs of the body, and
belongs especially to that group that are commonly
called emunctory—in other words, the cleansers or
purifiers of the blood. In this sense it ranges side
by side with the liver and kidneys; and, all things
considered, it would be a difficult problem for any
physiologist to solve, to determine which of the
three deserves to stand before the others in importance. These three organs are sometimes called
the scavengers of the body; and they may with
considerable truth be regarded as three great and
important systems of purification and drainage.

Now, if to drain the system of its impurities, to
cleanse and purify the blood of the animal economy,
three grand systems of drainage are required, the
inference is plain, that one would not be enough—
that two might perform the office, but with a strain
upon the machinery. But to be perfect, to perform
the office completely and efficiently, to be, in fact,
in health, to constitute health, all are needful.
Therefore, if in the course of these observations I
can show that one of these scavengers is weakened
in its powers, and being weakened in itself, throws

an additional degree of labour on the remaining two; if, in fact, our present mode of management of the skin tends to deteriorate its powers as a purifier of the body, and consequently produces a strain on the liver and kidneys, which leads to their deterioration and disease, I shall, provided I can also show that the bath preserves the health of the skin, make out a *primâ facie* case in favour of the bath.

But it is not as an emunctory or purifier only that we must regard the skin; its influence and power have a wider range of action in the maintenance of health. Besides comprehending a vast system of drainage tubes, which open on the surface by seven millions of pores, and which in actual measurement would stretch over nearly thirty miles if laid end to end; besides this, which belongs to its purely emunctory function; besides, also, a wonderful and perpetual labour, by which the skin is drawing from the blood certain organic elements in the fluid state, and converting them into solid organic formations, which are known as cells and scales, these cells and scales being the tesselated mosaic with which the skin is finished upon the surface, so as to render it capable of existence in the atmosphere of the external world; besides this, and much more, unnecessary in this place to detail, the skin is converted into a kind of sponge by the myriads of bloodvessels which enter into its structure—bloodvessels, that many times in

an hour bring the whole—ay, every drop—of the
blood of the body to the surface ; bring it that it
may furnish the materials for the microscopic pavement; that it may be purified by the abstraction
of its unwholesome principles; that it may breathe
the vital air of the atmosphere without ;—besides
this, also, the skin near its surface is one vast net-
work of nerves—nerves, mysterious organs, that
belong in their nature to the unknown sources of
the lightning, the electric currents of the universe.
And, besides these again, there is every variety of
animal tissue and contrivance by which all this
apparatus is held together and maintained in the
best state and position to ensure its safety and
perfection. In truth, the contemplation of the
structure and functions of the skin, when viewed
with the eyes of the mind, is almost overwhelming;
and as we gasp breathless, to gain an instant of
reflection, the words of the Poet break upon our
memory :—

> "In human works, though labour'd on with pain,
> A thousand movements scarce one purpose gain;
> In God's, one single can its end produce,
> Yet serves to second, too, some other use."

One word more as to the importance of the skin
in the animal economy, and that word a summary
of its functions and principal vital attributes. The
skin is a "sanitary commissioner," draining the
system of its impurities; it is an energetic labourer,
in that perpetual interchange of elements which in its

essence constitutes life; it is a regulator of the density and fluidity of the blood; it performs the office of a lung in supplying the blood with oxygen, and abstracting its carbon; it changes the crude organic elements of the blood, so as to render them capable of nutrition; it emulates the heart in giving speed to the circulating blood; it is the minister of the brain and spinal marrow in its properties of sensation; and it feeds and nourishes, and keeps in the highest operative condition, that part of the nervous system which is confided to its care. Viewing the skin in this way, and recognising its just claims to consideration as an important animal organ, we are led to the conclusion that the skin is a part of the digestive system, like the liver and kidneys, by virtue of its emunctory and nutritive powers; it is an appendage of the heart and a part of the system of circulation of the blood; it is a surface lung, a breathing organ; and it partakes of man's intellectual nature by its close connexion with, and dependence on, the brain. In the lower animals, the skin combines in itself alone, the feeling, seeing, smelling, hearing, and judging organ.

The structure of the skin—with its drainage tubes requiring a free exit; its streams of blood seeking for oxygen from the air; its nerves demanding the contact and stimulus of the atmosphere—obviously points to the relation which should subsist between man and the external world—to the fact that his natural and intended state is one of nakedness.

Certain portions of the skin, in different parts of the world and among different nations, are commonly exposed to the air as Nature doubtless intended the whole body to be. Our faces and hands; in women, the neck, and often the shoulders; among the Highlanders, the lower limbs; these portions of the body are naked, are unblushingly exposed; and, as we all know, without inconvenience. Who ever feared to take cold because his hands and his face were open to the free air of Heaven? What lady ever complained of inconvenience resulting from her *décolleté* shoulders at an evening party or the opera, or even from the bitter draughts of night air that frequently close those entertainments? Who ever heard of a Highlander suffering from rheumatism in the knees? That charming friend and companion of our youthful dreams, Miss Jane Porter, who was always taking colds from the slightest exposure of her skin to the air, once said to her brother, who was a physician,—"How I wish that my skin were all face?" "Try and make it all face," was his reply. And she partially succeeded; but for complete success she wanted the knowledge of the Turkish Bath.

The bath has the property of hardening and fortifying the skin, so as to render it almost insusceptible to the influence of cold. The feeling after quitting the Calidarium is one of defiance of cold; the bather has a longing for the cool air of the outer world, and with no other covering than his cotton mantle, a lawn or a terrace would be his chosen resort if the opportunity were within his reach. In the hands of Mr. Urquhart, the bath has presented us with one remarkable instance of the power of endurance of the skin developed by its aid. A fine, athletic child of five years old has been brought up in the bath, and has never worn other clothes than a loose linen garment. He is a sturdy little fellow, with the independence of deportment of an Indian and the symmetry of an Apollo. He was met one wintry day, when the snow was on the ground, walking in the garden, perfectly naked. "Do you feel cold?" inquired his interlocutor. "Cold!" said the boy, touching his skin doubtfully with his finger, "yes, I think I do feel cold." That is, he felt cold to his outward touch, but not to his inward sensations, and it required that he should pass his finger over the surface of his body as he would have done over a marble statue to be sure, not that he was cold, for that he was not, but to be convinced that his surface felt cold.

That the skin of man can support the temperature of a climate such as that of Britain, when trained to it from the cradle, is perfectly clear; our forefathers, the ancient Britons, wore no clothes. The Roman invaders of Britain tell us of the "naked savages of Scotland." The inhabitants of the Tierra del Fuego at Cape Horn, a country colder than Britain, have no other clothing than a hide which they hang on their windward shoulder; and their children may be seen, perfectly naked, gambolling on the sea-shore, and scrambling in the bottoms of the boats that come off to the passing ships. The mother of the little Apollo I have already described called the attention of a friend to the warmth of her infant's feet, and with the remark, "While my old nurse was with me, the child's feet were always cold, because she insisted upon covering them up with socks; but now that I leave them exposed to the air, they are constantly warm."

I need scarcely say more to prove that the bath gives endurance, and that endurance fortifies the individual against a very prevalent cause of disease in this climate—namely, colds and affections of the chest and lungs. A Doctor of Divinity whom I frequently met in Mr. Witt's Bath, told me that during the winter-time he was scarcely ever free from colds, often so severe as to lay him up for several weeks, and that he also suffered from attacks of neuralgia; but that, since he had adopted the use of the bath twice a week, all disposition to colds and neuralgia had ceased; and, for the first time in sixteen years, he had passed the winter without a cold.

It is impossible, therefore, to avoid the conclusion that the close clothing of the body from the moment of birth, and the continuance of the process through--

out our lives, must tend to prevent the proper and
healthy development of the skin and also to de-
bilitate it ; and that the opposite course, of exposing
the skin to the air, and promoting its natural
functions by means of the bath, must have the
contrary effect of hardening and strengthening the
skin and rendering its functions more perfect.

In the bath we learn to distinguish by the eye
and by the touch, the weak and the strong, the
unhealthy and the healthy skin ; we find the former
pale, soft, flabby, wrinkled, sordid, starved, and
morbidly sensitive ; while the latter is pink, hard,
firm, elastic, smooth, clear, sensible, and well
nourished. When the fingers are drawn forcibly
over the skin of the practised bather, the white
streaks caused by the pressure are instantly restored to their pink hue when the pressure is relaxed ; the sanguineous stream seems to follow the
pressure like a surge and instantly obliterates its
effects ; and the skin recoils with a snap like India-
rubber when it is pulled away from the body and
suddenly released. In the bath there are no
wrinkles and no decrepit age ; the skin becomes
firm and elastic ; it recovers its colour and its
smoothness ; it fits close to the muscular frame
beneath, instead of falling away from it in grim
festoons ; its hues are selected from the palette of
youth. But this is not all : as the skin regains its
health, the hair returns upon the scalp of the bald ;
and white hairs which have crept untimely and un-

bidden among the dark locks of mid-age, shrink away from the sight, and seek a more suitable and more unwholesome roost.

But these visual appearances of the skin, which obviously indicate its unhealthy external characters, also denote a deficient and imperfect circulation of the blood; a deteriorated sensibility; a defective cell-formation and secretion; an exhausted tone and vigour.

In respect of one of these qualities—namely, healthy sensibility of the skin—I met in the bath with a curious and unexpected illustration. When I was invited by Mr. Stewart Rolland to pass from his Calidarium at a temperature of 170°, into his Laconicum, in which the actual temperature was 190°, but the sensible temperature some degrees higher, in consequence of the presence of watery vapour, I was suddenly made aware that the skin of my body had lost its power of appreciating the higher degrees of heat, and that my face and hands were my only reliable monitors of the actual elevation of the temperature.

To the face and hands the temperature was for a moment almost scalding, but my body was sensible of no inconvenience. Had I been asked, before I made this experiment, what part of the body would have suffered most from the extreme heat, I should have said, the skin of the trunk of the body, because this is naturally the most sensitive from being covered and protected by clothing; but I was unprepared to find the real fact in the very reverse of this—to learn that the skin of the trunk of the body had lost its power of sensibility; in other words, had become partially paralysed from disuse of its proper functions.

In a word, the habit of clothing the body, of keeping it shut in from the air and from the light, weakens the nerves of the skin and consequently the natural and healthy sensibility of the organ. Although I could not appreciate the extreme heat of Mr. Rolland's Laconicum, I should have suffered acutely from a scratch, a pinch, or a blow on the bare skin : but the habit of the bath would reverse this unnatural sensitiveness, the skin would learn to appreciate truly instead of mendaciously; and blows, or pinches, or external injury, unless very severe, would cease to be felt as an inconvenience or an annoyance. The little boy bred in the bath complains of no hurt when he is accidentally struck or when he tumbles; and that which would be punishment to another boy is none to him. This, we see, must be the natural state of the skin, otherwise the Indian could no more exist without clothes than the lobster without his shell.

Another phenomenon of the bath shows the power of increased firmness and solidity and strength which the texture of the skin acquires by its use. A person unaccustomed to the bath bruises without any great force, and the discoloration of the bruise, occasioned by the escape of blood from its vessels and the dispersion of the blood in the texture of the skin, lasts for a considerable time. Indeed, we know of some skins that bruise upon the most moderate pressure, even without a blow. But the practised bather does not bruise, excepting from serious injury; and, when he does bruise, the discoloration is rapidly dissipated.

The power of influencing the skin by education is also shown in the degree of facility with which perspiration is induced in the bather. In the practised bather the perspiration comes almost at call; it comes soon, freely, abundantly: but in the neophyte, the perspiratory fluid is slow to emerge from its pores; it comes unwillingly and in insufficient quantity. Each succeeding bath, however, exhibits an improvement; and, in time, the perspiration obeys the word of command in the pupil as well as in the master.

I have assumed for the skin the possession of a power of nutrition, and have in this way brought it into the category of the digestive organs; let me explain:—Nutrition, in its essence, is that interchange of material, by the influence of which the old material is removed and new material is deposited in its place. Now, the emunctory function of the skin obviously results in the removal of the old material from the body, and in proportion to the energy and completeness of its removal, will be the eagerness of the tissues to take up new material

from the blood. If the skin be in the torpid and
atrophied state I have already described as the consequence of our present habits of life, this source
of interchange, of nutrition, will be valueless: but
if, by improving the health of the skin through the
agency of the bath, or by any other method that
can be devised, we render its function more active
and energetic, we necessarily make, nutrition also
more active and complete.

The accomplishment of this object is the basis of
that process known by the name of *training*, by
which animals are brought into the highest state of
condition and strength. It is for this that the racehorse is galloped, and sweated, and often purged ;
for this, also, the prize-fighter, the prize-rower, and
the prize-cricketer are made to go through a similar
ordeal. It requires little argument to show how ad-
mirably the bath is suited to this purpose; the sweating, the cleansing, the strengthening of the blood,
are obtained in the bath, without effort and without
exhaustion ; and the system is brought into that
state which, above all, is most favourable for the
absorption of new and nutritious material. The
bath has been already applied to the training of
horses, and before long will be used in the training
of men. The Romans kept their army in health
and strength by means of the bath; and the bath
might, on the same principle, be adopted with
advantage under all those circumstances in which

bodies of men are assembled together, temporarily or permanently, as in barracks, prisons, schools, factories, &c.

In the gas factories and metal-smelting houses, and probably in other trades where men are exposed to great heat, a plan is adopted which has considerable physiological interest, and is specially illustrative of the nutritive capabilities of the bath. In the retort-house, the stokers are kept for many hours in a deluge of perspiration; the drain is consequently very active, and it is necessary to supply the loss occasioned by that drain by means of drink. With this object, each man is allowed a certain quantity of oatmeal daily : the oatmeal is served out by the foreman, and is scalded with hot water and made into thin gruel; this is the drink with which the men supply the place of the perspired fluid. They give forth, in the shape of perspiration, water holding in solution the used and useless materials of the frame, and they receive in return a wholesome nutritive material. Can we wonder that these men are perfect Athletæ in form, that they are in the finest possible condition for labour ; and that, although working in buildings open to every draught of cold wind, and bathed in perspiration, they never, indeed they cannot, take cold.

Let us apply this lesson of the retort-house to the ill-nourished, weakly invalid; or, better still, to weakly, ill-conditioned children. Let us suppose that we have the power, by an easy, pleasant process, of extracting the old, the bad, the useless, even the decayed and diseased, stuff from the blood and from the system by means of the bath; how simple the operation by which we could give back in its place wholesome and nutritious material.— Where would be atrophy and scrofula, if we had this power?—and this power is, I believe, fast approaching, fast coming within our reach, by means of the Eastern Bath. We squeeze the sponge as we will; we replenish it as we will.

The faculty of preventing disease, as exercised by the skin, besides being indirect and operating on the general health of the body, is also direct. The skin repels the depressing effects of cold, of alternations of temperature, of extreme dryness or moisture, by virtue of its own healthy structure; by its intrinsic power of generating heat; and it also repels other causes of disease, such as animal and miasmatic poisons, by its emunctory power, which enables it to convey them directly out of the body. In unwholesome states of the atmosphere, in an atmosphere of malaria, which must necessarily pass into the body with the inhaled air, and being in the lungs must be absorbed by the blood, we naturally inquire by what means we escape the morbid effects of such malaria? The answer is :—the malaria is conducted out of the body as rapidly as it is introduced, by the emunctory organs—by the liver, kidneys, and notably by the skin. If the powers of the skin be weak, then the poisons are detained in the blood, and disease is the result; but if the skin be healthy and active, then they can do no evil; and ultimately they become innocuous. Thus the bath, by conducing to the health of the skin, becomes a direct means of preventing disease.

Reasoning, on the same premisses, shows us how the bath may be employed in the cure of disease. We can, at our will, so far excite the emunctory power of the skin as to make it the means of carrying off the elements together with the seeds of disease. If we wish to comprehend the operation better, we have only to watch Nature's own processes. A morbid poison is in the blood, it produces a shock to the whole system, that shock is represented by a chill; next to the chill succeeds a fierce fever, which marks the furious battle waged between the poison and the blood; then follows the perspiration, which hurries the contending poison out of the system; the perspiration, for the time being, is the cure. The observation of this well known series of symptoms suggested to the inventive mind of Mr. Urquhart the notion, that by raising artificially, as by the bath, the temperature of the body above fever-heat, the proper stages of fever might be stepped over; the chill fit would pass at once into the hot fit, and the hot fit be resolved by perspiration. The suggestion is worthy of mature thought.

Let me conclude with a brief summary of the sanitary views which it is my aim to inculcate in this essay.—I have endeavoured to show the importance of the skin as an independent organ endowed with sensation, circulation, powers of nutrition, and powers of elimination. I have viewed it in its relations to the rest of the animal economy—the digestive organs, the heart, the lungs, and the brain—with the purpose of showing its influence on these organs. I have regarded it in its natural state, as full of vigour, and possessing the properties of healthy colour, texture, sensation, and secretion; and in the unnatural state to which it has been brought by the perpetual use of clothing, wherein its colour, texture, sensation, and secretion are unhealthy, and its power of generating heat lost. I have explained the manner of operation of the bath on the skin, both in its healthy and unhealthy state; how, in the former case, it is a direct preservative of the health of the skin, and, through the skin, of the entire organism; and, in the latter, that it possesses the power of restoring the skin to a state of health: further, that the bath may be made the means of preventing disease, and an adjuvant in its removal when already established.

CHAPTER III.

RATIONAL USE OF THE BATH.

ADMITTING the importance of the bath to the health and well-being of society, when properly employed, it becomes our duty to consider in what the *propriety* of its employment consists.

It consists in the selection of a *temperature* which is suitable to the constitution and idiosyncrasies of the individual; of a *time of day* most in accord with the constitution of the body; of a period of *duration* of the bath; of the *frequency* of repeating it.

Then we have to consider certain points of detail which come before us in the shape of objections to the bath : for example, the apprehension of *taking cold* after the bath; of causing disturbance of the nutritive functions; of inducing weakness. And, again, we may view it as a remedy against certain affections of a spasmodic type, in which its mode of action is so clear as to be intelligible to the unmedical understanding; and further, we have to regard it in its applicability to our fellow-creatures of the four-footed class, and especially to the horse.

PROPER TEMPERATURE OF THE BATH.

The history of the Bath, together with its practice, so far as I have been able to comprehend it, both point to the Turkish Bath, as it at present exists in the East, as representing the proper standard of temperature. The Turkish Bath is a mixed bath of vapour and heat ; and although we have no information of its precise thermometric grade, yet we have sufficient data before us to be assured that the temperature cannot be high ; for we know, on the one hand, that watery vapour above 120° of Fahrenheit is scalding ; and, on the other hand, that the Turkish Bath is constantly taken by travellers and strangers ; and that inconvenience resulting from its temperature is an accident of the rarest kind ; so rare, in fact, as to be scarcely possible. Whereas, in the high temperatures at present in use in London, 170° and 180° of dry air, disagreeable and even dangerous symptoms are extremely common.

The great purpose to be arrived at, as far as temperature is concerned, is to obtain one which shall be agreeable to the sensations ; which shall slowly expand the pores of the skin ; which *shall produce perspiration gently and slowly and without effort ; so that it may be continued for an indefinite length of time.* The temperature of 135° or 140° is very agreeable to the sensations ; but in me it excites a perspiration which is too profuse ; the energy of perspiration occasions a feeling of exhaustion ; and the exhaustion is succeeded by quickened action of the heart, throbbing pulse, a sensation of faintness, of oppression, which makes it necessary that I should quit the Calidarium for a few minutes. It is true that these unpleasant sensations quickly pass off; but they are again renewed after a time, as often as I return to the Calidarium. It is easy to see why these disagreeable sensations occur; it is easy to understand, that the blood, suddenly robbed of a considerable proportion of its watery fluid, must, for the moment, occasion a physiological change in the whole economy. But we must do more than explain them to our own mental satisfaction, we must stop them; and the way to stop them is, I believe, to use lower temperatures.

Again, high temperatures clearly frustrate the purpose of the bath; by producing excessive perspiration, they shorten the period passed in the bath; they bring it to a too sudden and too rapid conclusion. Profuse perspiration is an excess of function, and excess of function cannot exist without fatigue and consequent injury to the organ so excited; together with more or less disturbance of the whole economy. I have had many complaints of the bath made to me, which have been clearly referrible to the use of high temperatures at the beginning of treatment; and the abuse is so plain, that I wonder, having once occurred, it could again be repeated.

These remarks point to the importance of a Tepidarium when a Tepidarium can be obtained; the time passed in the Tepidarium may be considerable, the body undergoing a gradual process of warming, of softening, of perspiration; and at the end of this process, being transferred for a few minutes only to the Calidarium.

TIME OF TAKING THE BATH.

The best time for taking the Turkish Bath, and, indeed, every form of bath, is that which is least likely to interfere with the process of digestion; for example, *before a meal.* But at this point it is necessary to draw a line of distinction between the Turkish Bath and all other kinds of bath: the Turkish Bath abstracts from the system a proportion of its solid constituents, more or less considerable, while it makes only a gasiform return in the form of oxygen. All other baths abstract little or nothing; and therefore, in this particular, there is a wide and important difference between them. It is as needful to take the sea bath before a meal as it is the Turkish Bath; but the sea bath may be taken before breakfast, which I should in nowise advocate in the case of the Turkish Bath. I do not mean that, to those who can bear it and who approve of it, the Turkish Bath might not be suitable on first rising in the morning; but the generality of mankind will find the most advantageous time for taking it from three or four, to five or six hours after a meal. At that time there will be that in the economy which nature can spare, and often with benefit to the health, the waste of the digestive process, the detrita of nutrition; whereas, before breakfast, there is or ought to be scant matter for giving off from the blood by way of perspiration. Invalids may take the Turkish Bath three hours after breakfast; or three hours after the midday meal or lunch; while the man of occupation may advantageously devote to its rites the hour and a half or two hours which immediately precede dinner; and the more engaged may probably, with equal advantage, take it in the evening, after the dust and toil of the day are at an end, and shortly before bedtime.

"Would it be no comfort, no pleasure, no benefit to an English lady, on returning from a ball, and before going to bed, to be able, divested of whalebone and crinoline, and robed as an Atalanta, to enter marble chambers with mosaic floors, and be refreshed and purified from the toil she has undergone, and prepared for the soft enjoyment of the rest she seeks?"*

DURATION AND FREQUENCY OF THE BATH.

The length of time spent in the bath must be regulated: partly by the object to be obtained; partly by the habits of the individual as regards the use of the bath; partly by his strength and powers of constitution; and partly by the temperature of the bath. The *object* of the bather may

* "The Pillars of Hercules."

be a moderate perspiration, or a thorough sweat; he may desire simply to evaporate from his skin the waste particles that occasion fatigue ; or he may wish to distil from his blood the morbid atomies of rheumatism, neuralgia, or gout; he may seek for the after enjoyment which follows upon a day's hunting or shooting ; or he may strive to gain the health-giving results of active exercise, for a body that has been immured in committee or in office all the day long. I have shown, in an illustration at p. 78, how the bath may be used for the removal of fatigue, of hunger, the cobwebs of the brain ; and how it may be made to fortify the powers of the muscular system and of digestion.

The practised bather will know when to cease the bath, without reference to other authority than his own sensations and experience. The weak and the strong must be equally guided by their powers of endurance, and all must be influenced to a greater or less extent by the thermometer. A bath at 180° cannot be borne for the same length of time as a bath at 130°; and it is clear that if a protracted bath be the object sought to be attained, the temperature must be moderate and agreeable to the sensations. In the baths of very high temperature the bather is forced to retreat before a full perspiration is accomplished, and he is therefore rendered liable to a secondary perspiration, which chills the skin and endangers catarrh and other local congestions, while he is deprived of the refreshing and exhilarating sensation which follows a properly-accomplished bath. For him, there is no jumping over a lamp-post, much less " the moon."

I have often passed an hour in the bath. Mr. Urquhart, Mr. Rolland, and Mr. Witt have spent several consecutive hours in the bath. Mr. Rolland lived in the bath for three days, quitting it only for a short period at a time. To some, a quarter of an hour in the Calidarium would be enough ; while others would prefer half or three-quarters of an hour. The Romans indulged in the bath to so great an excess, that it became necessary to pass a law to restrict its use to two hours. Dr. Millingen, Physician to the Sultan, in a letter from Constantinople, addressed to Mr. George Witt, observes:—"If a Moslem enters the bath for the object of a legal ablution, half an hour is amply sufficient ; if, however, a person wishes to go through all the stages of a complete bath, an hour, at least, or one hour and a half, is the usual time."

The frequency of taking the bath must, like other points of balneal economy, be regulated by the purpose sought to be attained. Where maintenance of existing health is the object, once or twice a week may be sufficient. I can conceive the bath to be made a part of the process known as " dressing for dinner," and then it may be taken as often as we dine. Medically, its frequency of repetition must be left to the medical man ; and in every case the amount of effect produced must regulate its repetition. " Little and often," I would suggest as a maxim applicable to the bath as to some others of the enjoyments of life; and much to be preferred to the opposite position, "seldom and much." The Romans took the bath daily; the Mussulmans take it once a week.

To the natives of a country possessing a damp, cold, and variable climate, like that of Britain, wherein catarrhs are the scourge of the population (such catarrhs being attributable in most cases to checked perspiration and extreme cooling of the surface of the body), the apprehension of cold and catarrh from the use of the bath is a natural expectation. But the practice of the bath proves such an apprehension to be unfounded, and our reason helps us to see that there is in reality no such danger. The ordinary process of taking a cold is as follows : we are warmed by exercise, perhaps somewhat exhausted at the same time; the skin is bedewed with perspiration; the perspired fluid evaporates, producing chill; and the chill occasions a shock to the nervous system and to the whole economy, that results in the reaction known as " a cold." But if we contrast these conditions with those of the bath, we find that there is no parallel between them. In the bath we perspire; in a warm and genial temperature we abstract from the system all the watery fluid that Nature has, at the time, to spare; we rinse off the perspiration with warm water; we shut up the pores by means of cold water; we warm the body anew; we then rest tranquilly until every particle of moisture is removed from the skin ; and when we are thoroughly dry, we put on dry and warm clothes. In this process it is clear that there is not even a chink by which a cold can approach us. If we hear of people taking cold after the bath, we may be assured that they have broken its laws somehow or somewhere. The bath, properly conducted,—and improperly conducted it is not the bath—THE BATH CANNOT GIVE COLD.

That which is most needful to impress upon nations unaccustomed to the bath, is a *respect for its ordinances.* People are apt, on their first introduction to the bath as a new idea, either to take alarm at the apparent severity of its processes, or to go to the opposite extreme of treating it inconsiderately. People require training to the bath, as they do to other processes which are calculated to affect the well-being of their constitution. If they were bred to the bath from their infancy, no training would be requisite; but as they are not, there are very few who can go through the London Turkish Bath in all its entirety, and as it is at present conducted, without risk of accident of some kind—that is, before they are properly seasoned. I call to mind a gentleman of susceptible constitution, whom I myself introduced to the bath: the temperature did not exceed 135° ; he felt very little uneasiness during the process ; but his liver took offence at the inordinate and unusual industry of its coadjutor, the skin, and was many days before its anger was appeased, the possessor being much troubled in the meantime by the intestine feud of his interior. But this affords no ground of argument against the bath; it only corroborates the views of moderation which I am endeavouring to inculcate. Had my friend taken the bath at a lower temperature, or reduced its duration to a shorter period, he would have suffered no inconvenience; and, after all, it was but the inconvenience attendant upon the initiation of a new physiological process.

A similar event occurred in the instance of another friend, a literary man, of sedentary habits, but thin, and not overcharged with waste humours. The temperature of the bath was the same, but my friend was not equal to the demand made upon his vaporizable fluids, and the use of the bath tended to derange his nutritive functions and lower his powers. Here, again, it was clear that a more moderate temperature, a slower transpiration, and a shorter period of duration, were the natural agents of cure. With these conditions there would have been no strain on the circulating or nervous system, and the bather would have enjoyed relatively the same advantages as another abounding in humours. If we had a choice, if we had the opportunity of selecting subjects for the bath, we should take them from the latter class; and these are the persons who would derive the greatest benefits from

its use. Another example of the abuse of the
bath was a lady who had taken twelve baths with
enjoyment and advantage: on entering the bath the
thirteenth time, the temperature was 190°, she felt
uncomfortable, and remained unwell for several
days. On the other hand, I have had the pleasure
of seeing many with whom the bath had disagreed
at first, become accustomed to it, and derive great
benefit from its regular use.

Non-bathers often express an alarm lest the bath
may be weakening. But the bath strengthens, it
never weakens, except, as in the instances above
narrated, it be used improperly. The idea of
weakening is suggested by the loss of fluids by
perspiration; but this loss is, as I have endeavoured
to show, a gain and not a loss. The expulsion of
watery fluids from the economy is a natural process,
necessary to our very existence, and without it we
should die. It would be very unreasonable to
regard the watery fluids expelled by the lungs, by
the skin, and by other emunctory organs, as a loss
of material necessary to the economy, or a loss which
could in any way affect the nervous and muscular
powers of the individual otherwise than beneficially
—unless, indeed, the loss be inordinate and excessive. Is it not one of the conditions of our
healthful existence, that we should earn our bread
with the sweat of our brow? and, writhe as we may
under the verdict, we must do so, or suffer the evil
consequences of a breach of Heaven's law. Mr.

Urquhart has the following observations on this subject :—

"There is an impression that the bath is weakening.   We can test this in three ways; its effects on those debilitated by disease, on those exhausted by fatigue, and on those who are long exposed to it.

"1. In affections of the lungs and intermittent fever, the bath is invariably had recourse to against the debilitating nightly perspirations.   The temperature is kept low, not to increase the action of the heart or the secretions; this danger avoided, its effect is to subdue, by a healthy perspiration in a waking state, the unhealthy one in sleep.   No one ever heard of any injury from the bath.   The moment a person is ailing he is hurried off to it.

"2. After long and severe fatigue,—that fatigue such as we never know, successive days and nights on horseback—the bath affords the most astonishing relief.   Having performed long journeys on horseback, even to the extent of ninety-four hours, without taking rest, I know by experience its effects in the extremest cases.

"A Tartar having an hour to rest, prefers a bath to sleep.   He enters as if drugged with opium, and leaves it, his senses cleared, and his strength restored as much as if he had slept for several hours.   This is not to be attributed to the heat or moisture alone, but to the shampooing, which in such cases is of an extraordinary nature.   The Tartar sits down and doubles himself up; the shampooer (and

he selects the most powerful man) then springs with
his feet on his shoulders, cracking his vertebræ ;
with all his force and weight he pummels the whole
back, and then turning him on his back and face,
aided by a second shampooer, tramples on his body
and limbs; the Tartar then lays himself down for
half an hour; and perhaps, though that is not
necessary, sleeps.   Well can I recal the hamâm
doors which I have entered scarcely able to drag
one limb after the other, and from which I have
sprung into my saddle again elastic as a sinew and
light as a feather."

Sir Alexander Burnes, in his "Travels in Bok-
hara," on the same topic observes :—" You are laid
out at full length, rubbed with a hair brush,
scrubbed, buffeted, and kicked ; but it is all very
refreshing."   And Anquetil gives the following
account of shampooing :—" One of the attendants
on the bath extends you upon a bench, sprinkles
you with warm water, and presses the whole body
in an admirable manner.   He cracks the joints of
the fingers and of all the extremities.   He then
places you upon the stomach, pinches you over the
kidneys, seizes you by the shoulders, and cracks the
spine by agitating all the vertebræ, strikes some
powerful blows over the fleshy and muscular parts,
then rubs the body with a hair-glove until he perspires, grinds down the thick and hard skin of the
feet with pumice-stone, anoints you with soap, and
lastly, shaves you and plucks out the superfluous

hairs. This process continues for three-quarters of an hour, after which a man scarcely knows himself; he feels like a new being.

"You will see a hammal (porter), a man living only on rice, go out of one of those baths where he has been pouring with that perspiration which we think must prostrate and weaken, and take up his load of five hundredweight, placing it unaided on his back.

3. "The shampooers spend eight hours daily in the steam; they undergo great labour there, shampooing, perhaps, a dozen persons, and are remarkably healthy. They enter the bath at eight years of age: the duties of the younger portion are light, and chiefly outside in the hall to which the bathers retire after the bath; still, there they are from that tender age exposed to the steam and heat, so as to have their strength broken, if the bath were debilitating. The best shampooer under whose hands I have ever been, was a man whose age was given me as ninety, and who, from eight years of age, had been daily eight hours in the bath. This was at the natural baths of Sophia. I might adduce in like manner the sugar-bakers of London, who, in a temperature not less than that of the bath, undergo great fatigue, and are also remarkably healthy."

THE MEDICAL PROPERTIES of the bath are based upon its powers of altering the chemical and electrical conditions of the organic structures of the body, and abstracting its fluids. The whole of

these changes take place simultaneously, and no
doubt harmoniously; but in certain instances we
may rely upon a greater activity of one of these
processes over the other two : for example, in neuralgia, the electrical power should preponderate ; in
the destruction of miasma and poisonous ferments,
the chemical power ; and in the slow removal of
accumulated morbid deposits, as in chronic gout and
rheumatism, the fluid abstracting power. The required greater activity of one or other of these
powers would also be our guide to those physical
conditions of the bath which are calculated to
effect these objects — for example, temperature
and moisture. The temperature and degree of
moisture for the treatment of disease must be different from that which is suitable to health. It
may be necessary to have recourse to very high
temperatures ; or it may be requisite to fall below
the healthy standard. Moreover, the healthy standard itself may require variation for different individuals and different constitutions. The physician
is perfectly conversant with this necessity of adapt-
ing his means to the special constitution or idiosyn-
crasy of his patient.

One of the most important properties of the
bath is its power of preserving that balance of the
nutritive functions of the body which in its essence
is health; in other words, preserving the *condition*
of the body. The healthy condition implies an
exact equipoise of the fluids and the solids, of the

muscular and the fatty tissues, of the waste and the supply. This state of the body is normally pre-served by a proportioned amount of air, exercise or labour, and food; but even the air, the exercise, the labour, and the food must be apportioned, in its kind and in its order, to the peculiar constitution of the individual. Those who have ever had occasion to reflect on this subject, must have felt the difficulties which surround it, and have been aware how extremely difficult it is to say what may be faulty in our mode of using these necessaries of our existence. If I were asked to select an ex-ample, as a standard of the just equipoise of these conditions, I should take the ploughman; intel-lect at the standard of day to day existence, moderate food, vigorous but not over-strained labour, plenty of air, and plentiful exposure. But who would care to accept existence on such terms as these. Give us brain, give us mind, however ungovernable, however preponderant its over-weight to the physical powers, however destructive to the powers of the body. In a word, we select a morbid condition : our meals, our air, our exercise, our indoor and outdoor habits are all unsound ; we prefer that they should be unsound ; the necessities of our life, of our position, require that they should be unsound. How grand, therefore, the boon that will correct these evils without the necessity for making any inconvenient alteration in our habits !

THAT BOON IS THE BATH. The bath promotes

those changes in the blood for which fresh air is otherwise needful. The bath gives us appetite, and strengthens digestion. The bath serves us in lieu of exercise. "The people who use it," writes Mr. Urquhart, "do not require exercise for health, and can pass from the extreme of indolence to that of toil." How glorious a panacea for those home-loving matrons whom no inducement can draw forth from their *Lares* and *Penates*, to enjoy a daily wholesome exercise, and who, as a consequence, become large, and full, and fat, and bilious, and wheezy; and who, in their breach of Heaven's law, lay the foundation of heart disease. "A nation without the bath is deprived of a large portion of the health and inoffensive enjoyment within man's reach; it therefore increases the value of a people to itself, and its power as a nation over other people."*

Dr. Millingen, in the letter to Mr. George Witt, previously referred to, makes the following interesting remarks on the bath, and offers an opinion of its importance, for which we were hardly prepared in a man living in its midst, and having its operation constantly under his eye. The prophet is clearly no less a prophet at home than abroad:—
"As to the application of the bath in the prevention and cure of diseases. The working classes among the Turks, for such classes do exist, and are as numerous and fully more hard-working than elsewhere, know of no other means of prevention,

* "The Pillars of Hercules."

on feeling indisposed, but the bath. In the numerous cases arising from sudden changes in the temperature of the body, a copious perspiration, which
a stay of more or less duration in the Calidarium
is sure to occasion, does, in the great majority of
cases, restore the body to the equilibrium of health.
After over-exertion, again, the bath is had recourse
to. In short, it is looked upon so much in the
light of a panacea by the lower orders, that they
hardly ever dream of consulting a physician when
taken unwell. If the bath fail to cure them, nothing else will succeed. This prevailing conviction
accounts, in a great measure, for the total absence
of dispensaries and civil hospitals, not only in this
large city, but throughout the empire. Yet I
apprehend, from the tables of mortality monthly
published, that the mortality is not greater than it
is in countries blessed with those institutions. The
higher classes, and women especially, do not, as with
us, know much about regular exercise, so that I
perfectly agree with you that, were it not for the
ample compensation afforded by the bath, they
would not enjoy the excellent health they generally
possess.

"You speak of the temperance of the people as
being pointed out as the principal cause of gout
being hardly known in this country. If this is
partly true, on the other hand I must remark that
intemperance of late years is much on the increase;
and, moreover, that it is carried on to an extent

L

which, if stated, might be looked upon as fabulous. Yet the gout is not more prevalent, nor delirium tremens either. This immunity I can attribute to nothing else but to the expulsion of the alcohol circulating in the system, by the lungs and skin, during the stay in the bath. You wish to know how long, on an average, does a person remain in the bath. If a Moslem enters the bath for the object of a legal ablution, half-an-hour is amply sufficient; if, however, a person wishes to go through all the stages of a complete bath, an hour, at least, or, one hour and a half, is the usual time.

" I consider that you are engaged in an attempt, which, if successful, will confer in an hygienic point of view, a service on our countrymen as eminent as the discovery that has immortalized the name of Jenner.

" We have not here the statistical returns indispensable to ascertain whether the medium range of human life is above or below the average in other · countries. Instances of extraordinary longevity are far from being uncommon. I have known, and know yet, several individuals among the natives more than a hundred years old."

My friend B—— is a man of leisure, so far as the common necessities of life are concerned; his worldly career has been successful; and, in gratitude to the Giver of mercies, he has devoted the remainder of his days to the service of God, to the doing of all the good he can to his fellow man; he is largely concerned in the management of public charities of all kinds; he is regular in his habits, active, and moderate in his diet; but, in spite of moderation, he is fat, and as a man who despises personal indulgence, his fat is an annoyance to him, and an incumbrance. "What can I do to become less bulky?" said he to me one day. "Go to the bath," said I; "and after the bath walk to your home in Kensington." "Impossible," said he; "Kensington is three miles away, and I cannot walk the length of a street without panting." "Have faith," said I, "and do as I tell you." A week after I received a note from B——: "I took the bath, as you desired me; after the bath I felt that I could walk to Kensington, or to Richmond, if I had chosen; but I had an appointment that obliged me to hurry home in a cab. Yesterday I took a second bath; I did walk home to Kensington, no less to my own amazement than that of my family; I ate my dinner with a relish that I had not known for years; and after dinner, the power and the desire to walk were so great that I could hardly repress them." B—— has continued the bath regularly ever since; he looks fresh and well, and more shapely; he knows no fatigue in walking; during the late severe winter he has required no great coat; in the midst of the bitterest frost he walked to the Serpentine in his shirt sleeves, with his coat upon his arm, and his clothing is now his only in-cumbrance. "I want to fit up a bath for the poor in my neighbourhood," was his remark to me at a late interview. "What convenience have you for the purpose?" said I. "A capital roomy cellar," was his answer. "Sell your wine, then," said I, "and make a bath." "Oh! I can give away my wine," was his rejoinder; "those who take the bath need no wine." Heaven's blessing on thy head, B——; thou art an honour to the name of MAN.

While on the subject of examples of benefit to the health resulting from the use of the bath, I may mention the case of a neighbour, by name Buckland, who has put up a bath in Westmoreland-street, Marylebone. Buckland was an upholsterer, but being seized with rheumatic gout, lost his business and fell into poverty. For fifteen years he was a cripple, and tried in vain, medical remedies, waters, and baths, one while taking the baths of Buxton, and another, drinking the healing waters of Wales. He then, by good luck, fell under the influence of Mr. Urquhart: by his advice he visited Manchester, and took several Turkish Baths there; he then returned to London and followed a course of baths at Evans's in Bell Street, Edgeware Road; and in 1859 he fitted his own bath, and has managed it ever since. He is no longer a cripple, but able to earn his own livelihood, and is an object of astonishment to those who knew him in the days of his suffering. The medical eye discovers that he is not thoroughly sound yet; but the degree of recovery which has already taken place is marvellous, and one instance

among many of the triumph of the Turkish Bath.
He has also had the good sense to discover the evil
of very high temperatures ; so that he is one among
the very few to whom I can conscientiously consign
the invalid.

There is a painful tension of the muscles known
by the name of spasm or cramp : like other complaints, it may be represented by a scale or ladder,
of which the lower bars are slight enough, but the
highest bring us to a knowledge of locked jaw, the
frightful spasms of Asiatic cholera, of tetanus, of
hydrophobia.   Heat and moisture are the well-
known and popular remedies for this state, and the
good woman of the house is always prepared in
such cases to recommend hot salt, the tin of hot
water, hot flannels, and flannels wrung out of hot
water.   These remedies are found to be useful, and,
being easy of access, are universal : a step above
these stands the hot bath, that *unready* remedy, that,
except in public establishments where it is in common use, is scarcely attainable.   For the relief of
spasm, the hot bath stands first among our external
and simpler remedies ; but miserable and wretched
indeed is the hot bath by the side of the Turkish
Bath.   In the hot bath it is a perpetual struggle to
keep your balance in the water, to keep the head
from going down and the feet from coming up ; the
head is kept above the water in a temperature different from that of the body, the neck feels cold
and damp ; the water is constantly varying in tem-

perature ; and last of all, you are lifted out of the
half-cooled water into the chilly air, to recover your
heat in a blanket the best way you can.   Perspiration in the hot bath is no sign of the state of the
skin ; the head seems to perspire, but it is probably
nothing more than the condensation of vapour on
the skin ; the perspiration of the rest of the skin,
if it occur at all, is lost in the water of the bath ;
and in the very outset of the perspiration, perchance,
the pores are chilled and a dangerous shock is com-
municated to the whole frame.   Well may Mr.
Urquhart exclaim :—"None but a Frank would
call a miserable trough of water a bath."

When, years ago, I prescribed for Mr. Urquhart,
while he was labouring under a frightful attack of
consecutive spasm, a hot bath, he gave me a practical lesson of the uses of heat and moisture, by
subjecting himself to a vapour bath of such a degree of intensity and duration as astonished all who
saw it.   The bath attendant whispered me that he
had never seen such a thing before, and relieved
himself from responsibility by saying Mr. Urquhart
"would have it so."   In fact, he had converted the
bath-room, for the nonce, into a Turkish Bath.   But
how miserable, how puny, how inefficient is the hot
bath, or the boxed-up vapour bath, to the free, the
open, the well-ventilated and well-heated Calidarium!   The sufferer from spasm may live in the
Calidarium, he may sleep there the whole night and
the whole day ; he may not only bring his muscular

system down to any degree of relaxation that he desire, but he may keep it in that condition for any length of time, or until the disposition to spasmodic tension has entirely passed away.

In a paper entitled "Thermotherapeia; the Heat Cure: or the Treatment of Disease by Immersion of the Body in Heated Air,"* I appended the following note as a convenient popular illustration of the action of the Turkish Bath in the relief of muscular spasm. "How many are the instances of spasm which come under the observation of medical men! Spasm of the stomach, of the bowels, of the ducts of the liver and kidneys, of the muscles. How needless to remind my brethren of their infinite variety; of their fearful agony; of our poverty of means for their relief. But here, again, the Turkish Bath cries out emphatically: 'Behold, we bring succour!' Without going more gravely into the matter, let us smile over the paragraph which I have just cut out of the *Cork Examiner*. As physiologists, we recognise the point and the value of the illustration; as philosophers, we appreciate the lesson, and become the wiser for its gift. 'One day last week, a boy, employed in Messrs. Simpson and Baker's biscuit factory was ascending to a loft, when one of the workmen below called him; and in turning his head quickly to answer the call, he got

* This Paper was presented to the British Medical Association, at its meeting in Torquay, in August, 1860, and was published in the " British Medical Journal" of Oct. 13th, 1860.

a crick in the neck of such severity that the head lay almost flat on the shoulder. The poor boy was going home in great agony, when he was met by Mr. Hegarty, the proprietor of the City View Turkish Bath, in the neighbourhood of Blarney, who, on learning what was the matter with him, sent him to take a bath. When the boy was inside about a quarter of an hour, and perspiration had set in, he was placed under a tepid shower-bath, and as soon as the water commenced to fall on him, the neck began to straighten, and in a short time the head had recovered its natural position, to the great delight of the poor lad, and rather to the astonishment of the other parties in the bath, who did not expect so speedy a cure. The boy was still suffering from a pain in the neck; but a second bath the next morning removed that, and he returned to his work immediately.'

"What remedy so potent for that dislocation and spasm of the fibres of the sterno-mastoid as the relaxing warmth of the Calidarium. How many who read this will call to mind hundreds of cases in which its effects to the untaught mind would be equally amazing. We may dare to balance its merits against those of chloroform. We may discover in it a valuable aid in the reduction of dislocations; in the relief of strangulated hernia; or in soothing the wasted pangs of parturition."

CHAPTER IV.

APPLICATION OF THE BATH TO HORSES AND CATTLE, FOR TRAINING, AND THE CURE OF DISEASE.

THE Turkish Bath is not only applicable to man, but is suitable also to animals, to the horse and the dog, those faithful and useful friends and companions of man ; and also to his oxen, his cows, and his sheep. In the instance of the horse and dog, it is capable of preserving health and condition, and preparing them by training for those feats of strength and speed which are peculiar to those animals. And it becomes an important and valuable medicine in treating their diseases.

In employing the bath as a means of training, we must have clearly before us the powers of the bath, on the one hand, and the precise objects which we wish to attain, on the other. The bath will abstract the old material from the system, and will thereby render the system more ready to take up and more capable of appropriating new and strengthening nutritious matter which may be given to supply its place. In other words, it will do the sweating part of the process excellently, without fatigue, without wear and tear to the economy.

But this, although a necessary part of the process of training, is only a part of the process. Other means are required to direct the new nutritive matter to the organs which especially require it—the organs of locomotion; and the principal of these means is exercise. The racehorse must still have his muscles trained by exercise; the prize-fighter, prize-runner, or prize-rower, must still pursue a systematic course of exercise; but the exercise in both instances is only that which is required to educate the muscles, to give them power, precision, facility of action, and to strengthen the breathing function; the exercise for the abstraction of unnecessary matter, for the removal of fat, is no longer requisite; for that the bath will amply and sufficiently provide.

My friend Mr. Goodwin, of Hampton Court, who has had much and the best kind of experience in the management of horses, tells me that for more than twenty-five years he has been in the habit of having his horses washed whenever they returned to the stable in a state of perspiration, and with the result that his stable was remarkable for the health and condition of the animals. His process was as follows:—the horses were thoroughly sponged over with warm water; then with tepid water; and, lastly, with cold; the water was then scraped out of their coats with a scraper (*strigillum*), and they were well wiped down with a leather. After this they were covered with a cotton sheet, and their legs were bandaged with cotton rollers. In fifteen or twenty minutes the sheet was raised gradually, first at one corner, then at another, until it was completely removed ; the uncovered portion being thoroughly wiped before the next was proceeded with, and the process being continued until the animal was completely dry. After this treatment, there was no fear of any subsequent *breaking out*, and however sharply the horses had been worked, frequently after a run at the rate of twenty miles an hour, they were ready and willing for a double feed of oats.

How different this picture from that of the common condition of horses under similar circumstances ; breaking out into a profuse, and often a succession of profuse perspirations after being put into the stable, and unable to eat their corn from faintness and exhaustion. But how curious the parallel with the stages of the Turkish Bath : the exercise is the *sudatorium;* then the operations of the *lavatorium;* firstly, the warm affusion, then the cold douche and the *strigil;* and, lastly, the *frigidarium* and the sheet. Nay, the parallel permits of being pushed even one stage further. My friend W. says :—" I have no objection to see a friend in the bath, or invite him to dinner ; but not both on the same day, for the bath makes him so hungry, that my cook threatens to give me warning."

Mr. Urquhart, in a note to " The Pillars of Hercules" observes :—" A plan has recently been suc-

cessfully adopted for drying horses after hunting.
Two men, one on each side, throw over him buckets
of water as hot as he can bear it; he is then scraped,
and rubbed with chamois leather, the head and ears
carefully dried with a rubber, and his clothing put
on. In twenty minutes he is perfectly dry, and
there is no fear of his breaking out again : the old
plan of rubbing him dry took from one to two
hours of very hard work, and he generally broke
out once or twice, and would often be found in a
profuse sweat at twelve or one o'clock at night.
The bath might be adopted for horses." " At present we shampoo our horses and clear off the epidermis, while we bestow no such care on our own
bodies."

On the application of the Turkish Bath to the
management and training of horses, the following
letter, addressed by Mr. Goodwin to the Editor of
Bell's Life, is especially important and interesting:—

" Mr. Editor,—I hope your insertion of Mr.
Erasmus Wilson's observations upon the advantages
to be derived from the Turkish Bath may be the
means of inducing owners of horses and their
trainers to try its effects. It is obvious that in the
racing stables such an adjunct must be found of
great use to horses whose limbs are defective, and
not capable of sustaining the exercise necessary to
reduce their superfluous flesh, and also in cases
where the constitutional powers of the animals in

preparation will not admit of their doing the strong work required of them.

"Mr. Wilson's remarks upon the system of washing horses after their work allude to a practice which was introduced, and successfully carried out, under my direction for many years in the Royal stables. The following narrative in relation to it may be some testimony in its favour :—When the late Earl of Jersey became Master of the Horse his lordship sent for me on one occasion hastily, to express his horror at seeing the stablemen wash a set of horses which had just come in from a sharp run on the Windsor road ; and so great was his lordship's prejudice to the innovation that I was afraid I should not be able to persuade him to permit its continuance, to give him an opportunity of observing its effects. His lordship, however, at my earnest request, came back to the mews in two hours' time to look at those horses, and not only found them quite dry and well dressed, but all of them eating their corn with good appetites. This induced his lordship to pay particular attention, whenever the opportunity occurred, to the horses so treated, and he became such a convert to this method, so new to him, that he often brought his friends to witness the beneficial effects of it; and, amongst others, the late Mr. Assheton Smith came, and immediately adopted it in his hunting stables, and, I have heard, with great success.

"I know not whether jockeys have ever tried the

hot-air bath for reducing themselves; but as they are compelled often to undergo such killing fatigue and privation as to impair their strength and endanger their health, they may, I hope, now that it is brought to their notice, be persuaded to make early trial of that which seems to offer them so much comfort. And as Mr. Wilson remarks that the skin of the accustomed bather perspires more readily and freely than in those whose pores have not been trained to its operation, jockeys may anticipate the acquisition of some very acceptable information.

"The expense of converting a loose box into a hot-air bath is so trifling that the experiment may be made at no great cost. London has already many Turkish Baths for bipeds, and I hope Newmarket will not be without one for quadrupeds. Col. Knox has testified to its beneficial results upon horses in Ireland; and Col. Towneley has one at his training stables at Middleham, which, I believe, has answered every expectation.

"In the treatment of disease I have often experienced the benefit of hot air; for in former days, when maladies in the horse were more rapid and acute than we now usually meet with them, and were generally ushered in by a cold shivering fit, it was my constant practice at Carlton House stables, when such a case occurred, to take the horse at once into the men's kitchen, and put him before the large fire which always kept it at a high temperature. By the heat, with the help of constant friction, I generally succeeded in cutting short the duration of the cold, clammy sweat, which is always indicative of mischief more or less serious. Were it for the treating of disease only, if I had a stable of valuable horses under my care, I would soon have also a hot-air bath.

"Yours, &c., W. J. GOODWIN.

"Hampton Court, Nov. 28th, 1860."

I have assumed for the skin the rank of a respiratory, of a breathing organ; and have endeavoured to show that the cooling and drying operations of the Frigidarium are an important part of the bath, as their performance is associated with the exposure of the skin to the atmosphere. Mr. Witt urges the prolongation of this period of the bath to as lengthened a degree as possible; and he delights to tell his auditors, dispersed around him like Roman senators in the Forum, and with no other garment than a cotton scarf, variously and negligently twined around their bodies—that this was the period when Pliny betook himself to his garden, and in the full light of the sun, and refreshed by the sweet breath of the unfettered winds of Heaven, walked in pleasant contemplation on a terrace carpeted with a beautiful little moss of velvet softness. We read that Sir Walter Scott indulged in this kind of atmospheric bath; we recognise in it the special charm and much of the

value of the river bath and the sea-shore bath ; and
we are not startled when we hear from the mouth
of an advocate of the Turkish Bath, Dr. John Le
Gay Brereton, in a lecture delivered in Sheffield in
1858, that—"After leaving the hot room in our
Bradford bath, bathers were in the habit, last
winter, of jumping into a bed of snow which had
been collected for the purpose. I have myself
spent the whole night in the woods at Blarney,
without any clothing save the bath-sheet, after
coming out of Dr. Barter's bath at that place. This
was after a ball, when, with several other gentlemen, we had retreated to the bath for the sake of
refreshment from fatigue. So delightful was the
cool air, that when far away from any dwelling, we
threw aside even our sheets, to enjoy the morning
breeze at daybreak. You need not then fear exposure to the air, after the bath ; it is not so much
for the sake of *cooling* that this process is necessary,
as to keep up the action of the bath by exposing
the skin to air ; it is to compel the skin to *breathe*."

The importance of *ventilating the skin* is illustrated in the process of clipping and singeing, as
applied to the horse. The thickening and length-
ening of the coat of the horse in the autumn season
is a change obviously adapted to prepare the animal
for the coming severity of the winter; and however natural in his wild state, is ill suited to his
condition as a useful and obedient servant of man.
As autumn advances, and after a few cold days, the

coat of the horse appears as if "broken up" into plots, and the individual hairs stand out roughly, or, in technical language, the coat "stares." Accompanying this change in the appearance of the skin, the animal becomes weak and languid, loses his spirit, breaks out into sudden and abundant perspirations upon slight exercise, and shows himself unequal to his work.   Now, the ready remedy for this state of things is the removal of the excess of hair, and the exposure of the skin to the action of the atmosphere.   If the coat be clipped close to the skin or singed, or, better still, be shaven, the animal preserves his strength and vigour, and is equal to all the labour that may reasonably be imposed upon him.   Of the three processes, shaving is the best, then clipping, and lastly singeing.   As to the latter, it is not quite clear whether its inferior position in rank to the others is due to the less complete exposure of the skin to the action of the air, or to the sealing of the ends of the hairs by the act of burning.   It is not improbable that the cut ends of the hair in shaving and clipping may serve as breathing pores for the inhalation of air, an advantage to the oxygenization of the circulation in the skin that is lost in the contraction and obliteration of the cells of the hair which ensues after singeing.

Another curious concomitant of clipping is the change in the colour of the coat, a change which seems to indicate that the colour of the hair produced in the winter time is different from that of the summer.

Dr. Barter, who has done so much to advance the popularity of the bath in Ireland, and has given much attention to farming operations, has applied the bath to the treatment of animals suffering under disease. The following extracts from a "Report of the Committee appointed to inquire into the Utility of the Turkish Bath erected by Dr. Barter, at St. Ann's, Blarney, for the Cure of Distemper in Cattle," have an interest peculiarly their own. Referring to one of the patients, the reporters observe : "We were informed she had been about an hour and a half in, had been eight days under treatment, and, as we were able subsequently to satisfy ourselves, had scarcely a trace of disease about her, and the next day was to be returned to the herd cured. She seemed quite to enjoy her position, the perspiration was rolling off her freely, and her breathing was slightly quickened. She carried her head erect, her eyes clear and healthy, and when she was removed to the outer room to get her douche-bath, no one could mistake the feeling or refreshment and pleasure that the dashing of each successive bucket of water over her seemed to give, and when she had been slightly rubbed down she was turned out to graze, the day being fine and warm ; but when otherwise, there is a shed close by into which the animals are turned after leaving the bath, to let them further cool and dry before being allowed out.

" One circumstance is worthy of remark, which applies to all the animals treated in the bath, and testified to by the men in charge of the four different baths we were shown—namely, the evident pleasurable recollection the bath seems to leave with them ; all the different animals—horses, dogs, cattle, and pigs—going of their own accord to the door of the bath, and dogs particularly indicating their anxiety by waiting at the door, whining till it is opened, and then running in.

" This finished our inspection, and we now beg to submit to your council the conclusions at which we have arrived from the above facts, and the information we were able to obtain in the course of our inquiries.

" First, the proportion of deaths to recoveries in the treatment of cattle distemper with the Turkish Bath does not appear to exceed one in ten, while the proportion that has been hitherto usual under other forms of treatment has varied from one death in three to one in four of the cattle attacked.

" Secondly, that the constitution is not impaired by the treatment with the bath as it is by any of the other systems with which we are at present acquainted ; and that this fact is particularly illustrated by the rapidity with which, in every case, the milk almost immediately returns on the animal being relieved from the disease.

" Thirdly, that in the treatment of several of the well-known serious diseases of the inferior animals, its use has been attended with the most favourable results, and particularly in all inflammatory diseases of the internal organs

" In conclusion, while we are far from thinking that a subject of such vast importance could be satisfactorily investigated in the very limited time we were able to devote to it, we nevertheless feel that we have seen and heard quite enough to warrant us in recommending the subject to the calm and serious investigation of those most vitally interested in the subject."

OBSERVATIONS ON THE USE OF THE BATH.*

A BATH is an aggregate of many parts, all more or less essential in forming the whole. To single out, therefore, any particular chamber, or any special contrivance used therein, and to call it *the* bath, is the same as singling out any room in a house, and calling it *the* house.

Bathing is a process; and that process is an elaborate one. It comes without thought to those accustomed to it, and no form of words can convey it to those who are not. The bath being the practice of a cleanly and polite people, habits of cleanliness and politeness must be observed by those who frequent it. No code of rules and instructions can teach the use of the bath: strangers must learn from the attendants how they are to conduct themselves, and not speculate upon what they do not understand. The following injunctions, however, may perhaps be of some service :—

I. The bath should be taken (especially by the uninitiated) before dinner: but if in the evening, a light repast may be taken in the middle of the day.

II. Habits of cleanliness, decorum and repose are imperative. The floors of the inner chambers of the bath must never be trodden with shoes; these, and all other ordinary articles of dress, are to be left in the outer room. The bathing dress is to be strictly worn through-

* These observations and rules for the bath were drawn up by a gentleman of much practical experience on the subject, and I have thought that I should be doing a service to the reader to reprint them in this place. They are peculiarly suggestive of self-management in the bath.

out, and never laid aside, except when the bather may be the sole occupant of an apartment. To ensure the necessary quiet and repose, all noisy and exciting conversation is prohibited.

III. Where there is a tepid-chamber, the bather is to remain therein for a short time, or until a gentle moisture appears on the surface of the skin.

IV. He is then to proceed to the hot-chamber (having first twisted a piece of linen around the head, in the form of a turban), and if, at any time, the heat be found oppressive, the head may be wetted with warm, and the feet with cold water; and he should pass to and from a cooler room, until the system becomes habituated to the heat. When the skin shall hereafter acquire a more healthy condition, and copious perspiration speedily results from every bath, the feeling of oppression will cease.

V. Water may be drunk, if desired; but to drink without the desire sometimes produces sickness.

VI. Shampooing (where attainable) necessarily precedes the processes of ablution, for which object the bather returns for a time to the tepid-chamber. In the absence of better means, rough linen or hair gloves may be used to remove the softened cuticle.

VII. From the hot-chamber he proceeds to the washing-room, if this should form a separate apartment. After the whole surface of the body has been well soaped and rubbed, it is to be exposed to a shower of warm water; and this soaping and cleansing is to be repeated as often as may be required. In all washings care must be taken that the same water shall never touch the body twice.

VIII. Immediately following the final ablution with warm water, the whole body should be subjected for a few seconds to a stream of cold water ; or the bather may take a plunge into a pool of cold water, where such convenience forms a part of the bath.

IX. If this application of cold be long continued, or if it take place in too cool a room, the bather should return to the hot-chamber for a few minutes, in order that the skin may regain its previous degree of warmth; generally, however (after having thrown aside the wet bathing garb), it will be sufficient to envelope the whole body quickly with a dry sheet, and to proceed at once to the—

X. Cooling-room, where the recumbent posture and perfect quietude are enjoined for a few minutes, until the accelerated action of the heart shall have quite subsided: the sheet is to be cast off by degrees, and its place supplied with a fresh bath garment.

XI. Plenty of time is to be devoted to this important department of the bath; the skin is to be exposed, as much as possible, to the vivifying action of the sun and air, and opportunity thus afforded to the newly-opened pores to absorb oxygen from the atmosphere. Where the cooling-room opens into a retired court, or garden, the open air is preferable.

XII. Before dressing, the whole surface of the body must be dry to the touch. If the cooling stage be hurried over, a secondary perspiration may break out; this may give cold, and this alone; but this is the result of mismanagement, not of the bath. Finally; the bather should "Dress deliberately, walk away slowly, and reflect properly on the blessing that he has enjoyed."

THE END.

LONDON:
SAVILL AND EDWARDS, PRINTERS, CHANDOS STREET,
COVENT GARDEN.